THE OBREE WAY

THE OBREE WAY

A training manual for cyclists

Graeme Obree

BLOOMSBURY

LONDON • NEW DELHI • NEW YORK • SYDNEY

Note

While every effort has been made to ensure that the content of this book is as technically accurate and as sound as possible, neither the author nor the publishers can accept responsibility for any injury or loss sustained as a result of the use of this material.

Published by Bloomsbury Publishing Plc
50 Bedford Square
London WC1B 3DP

www.bloomsbury.com

First edition 2013

Copyright © 2013 Graeme Obree

ISBN (print): 9781408196427

ISBN (ePDF): 9781408196441

ISBN (EPUB): 9781408196434

A CIP catalogue record for this book is available from the British Library.

Acknowledgements
Inside photographs courtesy of the author
Illustrations by Elliot McIntosh
Commissioned by Charlotte Croft
Edited by Nick Ascroft

This book is produced using paper that is made from wood grown in managed, sustainable forests. It is natural, renewable and recyclable. The logging and manufacturing processes conform to the environmental regulations of the country of origin.

Typeset in URW Grotesk and Rockwell by seagulls.net

Printed and bound by RRD South China

10 9 8 7 6 5 4 3 2 1

Contents

Foreword

John Beattie – broadcaster and former Scotland rugby international and British and Irish Lion

Growing up in Borneo as a small boy as the 1950s moved into the 1960s my heroes were all Scottish. My father would play bagpipe music on an old record player, my brothers and I would march around the bare floorboards to it, and he would tell us of great Scottish deeds as we gazed out at the steaming jungle.

Our dad was from Govan, a young rubber planter, but he spoke of the inventions, the peacemakers, some war heroes and of course the sportsmen and women. There was Jim Clark the racing driver, Benny Lynch the boxer, lots of football players and later Bobby McGregor the swimmer.

Even at that early age I think I understood that it was uncommon for Scots to be the best in the world at their particular sport, but if they got there then they had made a special sacrifice and they were very special men and women.

All through my sporting career as a rugby player I think I accepted that I wasn't the best in the world. At times I wasn't the best in Scotland, but that's what drove me and my friends to compete and sometimes come up with the most unlikely victories.

There is something distinctly Scottish about finding a unique solution to a problem and using it to win something.

The rugby victories came about through Scottish advances in sporting theory. Jim Telfer was ahead of his time as a coach, and fitness guru David McLean had Scottish players on fitness regimes before any other country had really started to do the same. We were given our own set of weights, our own training programme and tested on treadmills until we fell over.

For me, that information was like gold as I had been on a ten-year journey of discovery in trying to find the knowledge by reading great books – like those of Dr Danie Craven the South African – and phoning men like Bill Dickinson, the first 'advisor to the captain' in Scottish rugby, long before coaches were invented.

That has always been my fascination with sport: it's a constant search for knowledge. Sport is for everybody, and each and all of us want that knowledge presented simply and effectively. And that brings me to Graeme Obree.

Graeme is known for putting himself on the line. His manual is a continuation of this trait as Graeme gives away 45 years' study of the bicycle and the athlete. Like an Ayrshire Confucius he knows his own mind, body and his relationship with his sport in infinite detail – close to obsessive compulsive but also with a vigorous intellect to drive the passion and enable a really holistic investigation into the correct path for him. This does not entail that he is *always* right, as this is not the case, rather that he is prepared to search for the better solution to enable improved performance.

Like all great sportspeople he knows his craft intimately, everything he can consume about cycling, aerodynamics, physics, force, athletic performance he has consumed in abundance – in the words of another Scottish cycling great, Robert Millar – he's got the T-shirt.

The Obree Way is a one-stop shop for all cyclists, particularly those with a new or renewed passion for the sport, and contains a huge breadth and depth of knowledge and understanding. But it is written for the layperson – like a novel, not jargon laden, not trying to sell new improved products.

This training manual is different. It makes the complex simple and is for the social cyclist as much as the elite. As you read it you can hear a great mind at work, thinking the issues through. Issues easily applied to sports other than cycling.

And the tips laid out in this book made him great. The knowledge here is extraordinary.

You know, somewhere, when Graeme was breaking world records, fathers would have been telling their sons about Graeme Obree, the Scot who was the best in the world.

Oh, by the way, one of those fathers was me.

Introduction

When I joined a cycling club at the age of fifteen I had no idea that I would go on to become a world champion and world hour record holder. At the start I would ride about in jeans and a padded jacket and had no interest in competitive riding, captivated instead by the thought of the next horizon.

I was fortunate that I landed in a position where I would learn a lot from the start about the two main aspects of cycling – the equipment and the physical demands of the sport. Not having loads of cash to spend meant that I had to be very hands-on with old, recycled or damaged equipment, but that was an excellent way to learn what you do and do not do in regard to bike set-up. I ended up involved in racing pretty quickly but at the same time undertaking huge rides through the Scottish countryside with experienced riders, and that kick-started a learning process that would only continue.

Using a pre-Second World War track machine and a combination of (then) contemporary training ideas alongside my own ideas I became Scottish Junior champion in 1983. It was an era when the concept of getting in as many miles as possible was being challenged by new ideas about speed work, interval training, strength work, etc. In a vacuum of real awareness I found it necessary to employ training methods that I felt worked for me and that survived the process of logical analysis.

In the following years it would become habit for me to question every aspect of bike set-up, riding technique, positioning, nutrition and training. This led to the development of the ski-tuck position in 1986 that I used when attacking the world hour record on Old Faithful in 1993. Those intervening years were filled with analysis of many other aspects of racing and preparation that cumulatively have a large effect on the efficiency of the cyclist.

For me that meant not only using the tuck position but also employing a lot of additional knowledge, information gained through experience, experiment and – in a lot of cases – failure. The day I broke the world hour record, I stepped up on a bike that is now famous for being partly constructed out of a piece of a washing machine, Old Faithful, but what people did not see was the pedalling technique that maximised efficiency as well as the breathing control, as best as I knew it at that time. Also not seen is the belief in my own ability that did not come naturally from my own personality but from the realisation that without using the power of the mind it is not possible to achieve optimal performance.

Having dabbled in other sports like speed skating and triathlon in the 1980s and having experimented with alternative training approaches, I developed an almost obsessive need to drill into information sources in an effort to determine 'best practice'. This meant analysing every detail of every system, some traditional and some commercial, the commercial systems of course driven by the need to sell products and services. To focus my understanding, I absorbed as much information as I could from textbooks and research, while at the same time not losing touch with whether something 'felt right'.

After gaining the world hour record and winning the individual pursuit title in 1993, my tuck position was banned. I had no choice but to use these very same techniques of analysis to maximise the potential of the clip-on 'tri-bars' that the other riders had been using all the while. The result was the 'Superman' position with my arms stretched straight out in front. I regained my world title using this style and it was copied with great success by other riders, but it was banned soon after.

I carried on riding conventionally, and using my training knowledge I won the British National Time Trial Championship in 1997 as a point of proving athletic rather than technical advantage. I have raced sporadically over the years with reasonable success, and since I do not possess a car I have maintained my interest in cycling performance. Further study allowed me to enhance my breathing technique and pedalling style, and I have a body of knowledge that I wish I had possessed much earlier in my cycling career.

What I put forward in this book is in effect my own modus operandi. This is a time of great popularity in the sport of cycling and there can be a bewildering bombardment of advice to trawl through – especially for those new to the sport – and much of it is quite contradictory. You may or may not find every piece of advice in this book useful, but what I offer up is the totality of my own ways, no more and no less. I have tried to be as objective as possible, but where a statement is purely opinion I have tried to make that clear. I hope the advice is of use and can make a difference to readers in some small way.

01

What is training?

Training is bad for you! Training followed by rest and proper nutrition is good for and will make you better prepared for the event you are training for. I set out from the start to shift the emphasis and importance put into the physical act of training that exists in the sporting world. I prefer to put that emphasis instead onto the end product, which is being better prepared for your sport, mentally and physically, than you are now. In other words you have to think of training as just one step in the process of improvement.

I have seen it even at the highest level of sport where the training mentality has led to fatigue and diminished performance and sometimes injury and illness. Science has a term for this: the law of diminishing returns, the point at which output exceeds return. This training mentality is admirable in many ways as it shows commitment, work ethic and ambition. However, a commitment to work as hard as you can for as long as you can is brilliant if you are building a house or running a business, but not if you want to be in the best shape for your event. It is an attitude that is so universal and ingrained that it is very difficult to turn around, even in individuals whom I know and see regularly. The importance of this enlightenment cannot be overstated, and that is why I chose it as the first message on the first page of my training manual.

OK, work ethic and ambition are good, but only if they are directed and used while producing the physical effort you need to in order to improve. To truly utilise this new attitude to your benefit you will need another quality without which real improvement will not materialise – confidence. You need total confidence to know you are right to train differently or not at all on any particular day when your work ethic, logic and friends pull you in a different direction. Let's face it, it is commonly accepted that the more you put into something the more you get out in terms of results. And it is counter-intuitive to normal practice whether it is work, business or playing the piano that doing less gets more. I'll talk more about confidence in Chapter 6. For now you will truly need to believe in the new concept, that the physical act of training is almost an unfortunate necessity in the process of improvement in order to really carry it through.

Here is one analogy I like to use. Suppose you took up gardening and began by digging a huge allotment. At the end of the first day you have developed blisters but doggedly continue in the belief that the more digging you do the more your hands will adapt. At the end of a few days your hands would be a complete mess, blistered beyond short-term repair. Let's imagine your identical twin had done the same except only dug when his or her hands had healed, then their skin would be better adapted to the digging – with less digging! Suppose the object was tougher skin and not how much hard digging you could achieve then it is clear that you would get more results for less effort.

OK, so you have got the idea, but here is another point about training taken from that same analogy. The net improvement as cyclists by digging has been marginal if any. The net improvement in digging has, on the other hand, been the biggest single thing that has been improved by the digging. You may think this is obvious, but let's put it in the real world of sport. Rolling about on a Swiss ball will, more than anything else, make you better at rolling about on a Swiss ball. I will say again in relation to energy drinks and the like – there is a lot of commercial drive to promote new and improved training ideas and products, and it is important to point out that magazines and books benefit from promoting these new and improved training products, as they can help make the magazines and books more interesting. What I am saying is be wary of articles and the like telling you to buy this or that product or to train in a particular way. Often the commercial benefit to the seller is greater than any likely return to the buyer. Now, this book is also commercial, it comes with a cover price, but in reality I am dispensing with commercial sponsorship (not for the first time) and bringing you the truth as I have analysed it and used to have the success I had in my career. Success I would not have enjoyed had I listened to the advice of the day, which was to get a lot of miles in.

I am happy to admit that doing 'Swiss ball' will improve cycling performance to some degree, just as digging the garden or stripping wallpaper will improve cycling ability – when compared to doing nothing at all. If I was a tennis player and wanted to improve by playing snooker, then there would be marginal benefit through hand/eye coordination, but then doing Swiss ball would be better, but then again doing tennis would be the best option for improved ability.

To take it further may I suggest that although playing tennis generally will improve your serve, practising your serve is the best way to improve your

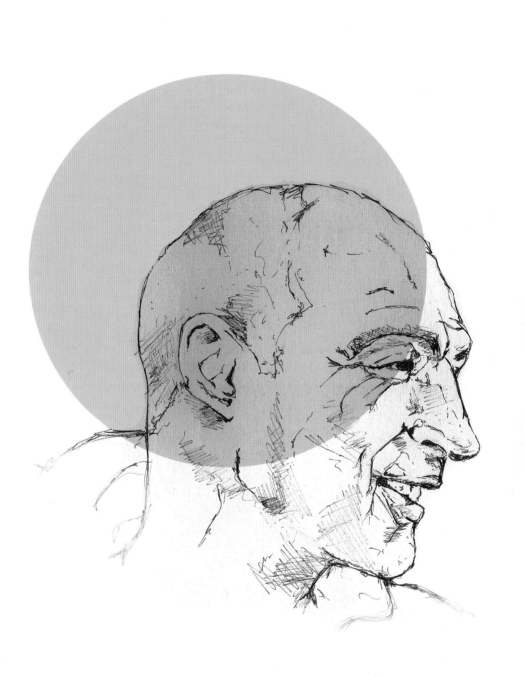

serve. Let me take it even further. Practising your serve in a competition environment is ultimately the best way to improve a tennis serve in the competition environment, which is after all where it matters. To put it in clear terms, training is an activity that is undertaken to improve performance, through the recovery process, at the activity undertaken. More than this, it is the first step in a process of physical and mental adaption to the intensity, duration and type of effort made during the training activity and within the spectrum of the sport itself. In relation to cycling I have to make it as clear as possible that the activity of cycling will improve every aspect of cycling performance once recovery has taken place, but cycling at intensity, pedalling rate and duration of your chosen event is the most effective way to improve performance at that discipline within the sport. Specific training for specific results. Everything else is peripheral and less effective than the base truth of athletic performance enhancement.

My idea of training in any field of endeavour whether it be music, sport or whatever else is an activity that once it has been completed, including recovery, makes you better at that activity than before you underwent 'training'! Training is also the long-term process of physical effort and recovery over the course of time that leads to a significant improvement through a series of increments.

Training, for many people, is a lifestyle choice almost like a hobby in itself. I see this regularly especially among those who tend to always train with groups or clubs where training sessions are usually pre-planned and set to a schedule based on days of the week. This is not the best way to optimise your potential improvement for more than one reason.

Firstly, the routine takes no account of your personal recovery from the previous ride. This means that if you're not fully recovered then you will not be able to ride harder or longer than the last time, so not only will you forgo the opportunity for improvement but you will be tired and therefore set back by a number of days before you can set out for optimum improvement.

Secondly, group training on the whole tends not to be specifically targeted at specific events, and individual goals tend to be amalgamated into a group average. Also, more able riders tend to get less out of group riding since there is an element of mercy towards weaker riders.

The positive aspect of group training is the sociability and enthusiasm that these groups have, especially at club level. I have always been a member of an amateur club and found effective ways of maximising my training without losing touch with ordinary members, even when competing at world level. It has to be said that although there is a lot that can be done to dovetail a personal and specific training need into a group ride, there are times when a choice has to be made between the optimum training ride and the camaraderie of the club ride.

The entire process of training is aimed at physiological and psychological adaptation. The largest part of adaptation is physiological, of course, but I do have to point out that the thought processes needed for specific physical efforts will also be strengthened. These are the neurons and signalling pathways that tell what muscles to move and when. It also ought to be pointed out that unless a training ride achieves a level of stress high enough to cause physiological improvement then it is not in fact a training ride. That would instead fall into the category of riding kind of hard. This is actually the worst kind of riding to do as a general policy to improve your performance as a cyclist. It is a great idea if you have just taken up the sport in terms of riding skills and general development, but if you cannot make it stretch you in terms of endurance or pace then it falls short on the basis that it is a wasted opportunity and also that it may not be hard enough to take the edge off a proper full-out ride the next day.

training, more than anything else, is very repetitive

In my career I spent many summer evenings on a static bike rather than out on a ride with others. Which brings me to the next point, which is that training, more than anything else, is very repetitive. By its nature of incremental improvement it has to be, and if you add the need for specific training for a specific result then it becomes even more so.

Repetitive training is therefore dependent upon a mind to perform this regimented series of training efforts. Loss of motivation through boredom of repetitive efforts is one of the largest causes of underperformance. The mind, for that reason, must be included in the overview of training, and in a way it also must be trained to be a 'training' mind. I'll get back to this one in Chapter 6.

The human body can be described as much as anything else as an electrical device and the training process will strengthen the parts of the brain that direct muscle movement as well as the signalling pathways (nervous system). These can also be improved when not actually riding, but again that is for later chapters.

The physiological adaption of the muscles and energy systems takes place as a result of what happens *after* an appropriate training effort has been made. To reinforce the idea that that first step to physiological improvement in your ability to cycle is just that, a first step, let me point out an important fact about any training effort. A training session leaves you *less* able as a cyclist than before you undertook that effort. As soon as you have finished a serious effort it is obvious to anyone who has ever done any physical sport that you are less able to immediately repeat that same effort. Clearly you are likely to have tired muscles and diminished energy levels. As I stated at the start, the immediate result of training is bad for you in terms of your ability to undertake that same effort again.

I labour the point so that I can talk about the part of the training process that is good for you and makes you more able to cycle than before. This is the physiological adaption that takes place under the right conditions of recuperation and nutrition.

It has been a necessity for survival for higher organisms that they physically adapt in response to the environmental conditions that they find themselves inhabiting and the stresses such conditions put on them. This adaptation not only restores the body to its original condition but can, given adequate time away from that stress, become stronger and more stress adapted than before. This effect is conditional, though, in that the adaption only takes place in relation to the specific stress involved.

> having the confidence and belief and trust in what your own body is telling you will be the biggest challenge you will face in your training

In relation to cycling then, the specific environmental stress is the need to pedal so hard for so long at a certain pedalling rate. The adaption period is the time after this when rest and good eating allows an improvement beyond the original ability. It has to be said also that removal of the stimulus to adaption (physical training) will, after complete recovery, lead to the gradual loss of that adaption (form).

From all of this we can see that there is a period after physical training where it is in the cyclist's best interest not to try and stimulate any further adaptation since this would retard the incomplete adaptation already under way (still riding about is OK if done at a low enough intensity). We can also see that after a certain time the adaptation is complete and will start to diminish and that further stimulus (specific training effort) is required in order to carry on the long-term improvement in cycling ability.

Well done if you are already wondering when the optimum moment is. This is a complex issue and varies from person to person and type of training done. It even varies for one individual from week to week. For me I might recover totally in two and a half days one week or four days the next. I will cover all of this in more detail later in the book but for now just hold the thought that the training effect is specific to the training stimulus and that complete recovery is vital to improvement (overcompensation).

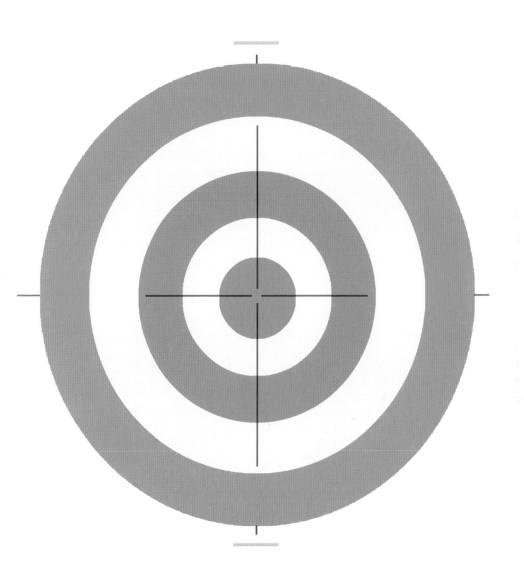

The balance between recovering to the same ability as before or into the zone of improvement is dependent on patience and the confidence to continue in recovery mode. Most cyclists I know usually fear that they have gone past full recovery and that they have entered the phase of losing their condition and as a result set out on another training ride prematurely. The result of this is that because they are not fully recovered they are only able to ride 'as hard' as before. Not only does this rob them of the opportunity to reach a new personal level of performance, but if this behaviour continues then the 'plateau' syndrome kicks in where no long-term gains are made at all. There is a common syndrome where athletes see a lack of improvement and being work-ethic influenced and focused on training they increase the volume of hard efforts. The net result of this is even worse. I knew one rider who, at the end of the process was diagnosed with exhaustion and malnutrition.

Having the confidence and belief and trust in what your own body is telling you will be the biggest challenge you will face in your training. It is easy to read and I think it makes good sense, but in the real world when the sun is shining and you are thinking about the event coming up, it goes against everything we are, as dedicated athletes, to go softly, softly one more day.

The graph below shows roughly the cycle of training recovery. I have deliberately omitted inputs.

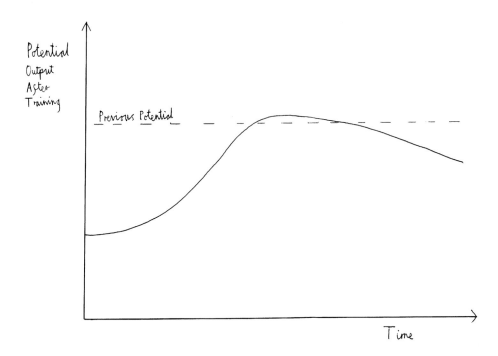

You can see from the graph that there is a period of time when an improved ride can be made. The tail-off is longer than you may have imagined. In other words, if you have a constraint of work, family, social situation, etc., then it is clear that it is better to be a day late with a proper stimulus effort than a day early. You can also see that there is an optimum point of when to train again at full strength for the best improvement in the shortest period of time. I'll come back to this one in more detail but I can assert that when the vast majority of athletes think it is now – it's tomorrow!

IN BRIEF

Training is an activity that is undertaken to improve performance. Finding the right balance between the training and recovery cycle is vital to allow the body to achieve full potential or as near to it as is possible. Also, think about the activity you are training for and tailor your training effort to meet the effort needed for that event.

- **Training is a long-term process**
- **Training is repetitive**
- **Training is physiological**
- **Proper recovery is vital for improved performance**
- **To reach peak condition it is necessary to learn to listen and respect your body**

First steps

What you will read in this chapter may seem complicated and confusing. Please trust me – I write this book to bring you a training system that gives the best results with the least amount of wasted time. The end result when you are set up to go is simplicity along with clinically controlled improvement. The endeavour, this passion of yours, need not be haphazard and all-consuming in time and effort. Think of this chapter as a guide to setting yourself up to be businesslike and efficient in your quest. Setting up for any serious endeavour, there has to be periods of effort to put in place the infrastructure that then allows for efficient operation. I offer you clinical and businesslike analysis which will lead to direct performance improvement, but I make no apology that it first requires effort from you.

The first and most important piece of advice I give to anyone who wishes to improve in the field of cycling is to get set up with a proper static trainer. It does not matter if you are a triathlete, road racer, time-trialist or general sportive rider. I say this because a fundamental truth about an aerobic sport like cycling is that how well you can perform is closely related to your aerobic threshold. My definition of this is basically how much energy you can output in a one pace effort – a no frills, no stops and starts, all-out effort for 20 or 30 minutes.

Clearly the limiting factor in this effort is how hard you can breathe in that period to supply the oxygen that your muscles demand and your physiological ability to endure the sensation of hypoxia (out of breath/ suffocation). Everybody has an aerobic threshold and improving it requires small increments in the output power in repeated efforts over a period of time. In order to achieve this any increment must be measurable, reliable and readable in real time to the rider so that they can see instantly whether you must speed up or slow down a little to be on target for a new level of straight-line output. I will talk about the actual training requirements in Chapter 4, but for now it is vital that you realise that this piece of equipment, along with the statistics that it builds up over months and years, will be of supreme importance.

In my professional days it would have been the first piece of equipment I would have saved from a fire so please take this mission very seriously. Reaching your full potential will be almost impossible without it.

It may be that you possess a turbo trainer or static-bike set-up already but please read on. I have rarely come across a set-up that would satisfy my standards of reliability and repeatability over a long time frame. Even then, the ones that were satisfactory were so only on condition that the levers and setting never be touched and the entire unit never be moved for fear of change of resistance or calibration – not ideal. The problem with most machines that I have seen is that where there is a cable adjustment the problem of cable stretch and wear takes away the possibility of accurate repeatability. There is a similar problem with electronic calibration as well. To complicate things even further there are different ways of creating resistance, but I would only rely on one of them to remain unchanged over time. So let me explain what we do want.

What you will need first is a bike to mount onto your rig when you have it ready to go. The prime requirements for this is that it *must* have the same length of cranks as you race and ride on. Read about this in other chapters before purchasing any more kit that includes cranks. As a good guide for now your crank length should be about 9.5 per cent of your height give or take a handful of millimetres either way. In terms of gearing, the set-up must allow relatively low gears, for a very easy to harder progressive warm-up, ranging to a mix of higher gears. It is essential that the largest of these should be close in ratio to ensure you are pedalling at your optimum rate during your effort. It also *must* be able to allow the saddle to be in the exact position, relative to the bike, that your race and riding bikes have. It also has to have a 22 or 23mm HP tyre (not tubular – the glue-on kind) that will take a pressure of at least 120 psi/9 bar. You can buy special turbo tyres but I have never had any problem with standard tyres. I also recommend you buy one extra exactly the same and store it in a cupboard for later years. Future seasons are something we tend not to plan for, but when you have a tool that can tell you exactly what pace you have to achieve to replicate previous results it is good policy to have like for like. To this day I have a logbook with my training sessions and race results as well as the preset turbo *and* the exact tyre. What I own is a personalised tool that will tell me exactly how I would perform on the track or road against previous results. More to the point it can tell me exactly what I must do in order to achieve a stated goal. This will be your tool too with a good set-up. The handlebar set-up on your turbo bike is not so important since the general lack of lateral (side to side) movement in commercial machines means that you cannot properly replicate a road ride anyhow. Lateral movement has crept into the commercial machine market but the first and by far the most important factor is accuracy of repeatable rides by the methodology I will explain.

The bike also has to be fitted with a rear wheel sensor computer with the display right in front of you in the middle of the handlebars. Make sure your computer is set to your 22mm or 23mm tyre size and to kilometres per hour, and also make sure you get a model that has a stop facility that freezes your data at the end of your ride. By that I mean you press one button to totally freeze your data while you are still pedalling. All of the above can be done by a good independent bike shop if you are not very technically minded. I should point out that using your race or riding bike is absolutely fine, perfect even, since it has your exact riding position. The advantage as well is that you will have one less bike to buy and store. The downside is that it has to have that rear mounted computer, and also you have to be prepared to fit your turbo rear wheel in every time you do a session.

The rig itself or 'turbo trainer' as it is usually known in cycling speak is the most challenging part of your mission. If you own one already and it says 'fluid' on it, then in my opinion and experience it is a fine trainer – *but* – it is not accurate enough from ride to ride, let alone season to season. It does not matter how expensive or fancy it is or how many functions it has, it still holds true that the resistance is dependent on a fluid being thrashed about and that resistance is related closely to the viscosity of the liquid that is variable by temperature. That temperature cannot be regulated since your energy during the ride heats it up and the ambient temperature plays a part as well. To appease manufacturers and to reassure you, I can honestly say that they are very reliable and long lasting – they just are not consistently accurate to 0.01 per cent deviation or as near as possible for our purposes. If you do own one of these already, then it will not go to waste since you will want to have a turbo upon which you can warm up at events. And you would not want your accurate rig being taken out and about. I do have to point out that the accuracy I seek is not measured against any other turbo trainer or any scientific measure of energy. It is an accuracy that be relied on when compared to every other ride you have done on the same turbo. What we end up with is not only a tool that allows you to measure a series of micro-improvements but a personal index that we can compare against actual performances.

There are some other main types of resistance generation. There is belt round a wheel (not many these days), magnetic, air fan, or quite annoyingly a combination of them. What you are looking for is a magnetic – and just magnetic – resistance turbo. It is quite common to have magnetic turbos with an air fan as well. If you own one of these, then the fan can usually be removed fairly easily. The reason that air fan resistance is not good is similar to the problem with fluid where temperature affects the resistance. There is the added problem of atmosphere air pressure that can vary by a range of up to 10 per cent as a result of high and low pressure weather systems coming and going.

The bottom line is that what you need is a simple fold-out magnetic-only turbo that has as few features as possible. Extra features are not a problem as such, but we will absolutely not use them so it is more a case of paying extra for gimmicks that I will ask you to remove or ignore anyhow. It is worth looking at the construction of the turbo and especially the clamping system and making good judgement about the cumulative wear that it will endure over the course of time – be a bit sceptical and wary of plastic parts. It is also worth looking at the barrel that the wheel runs on since the larger, the better. It is worth paying a little extra for this, and if it means you get a more substantial magnetic unit as well, even better.

A lot of people reading this might live in accommodation that requires you to undo your turbo each time you use it. That is absolutely fine and provided you make sure the clamping system looks reliable over time then no problem.

There is just one other feature you have to be sure of when assessing your current turbo or buying one. Make sure the roller that runs onto the back wheel is spring loaded – steel springs pretty much hold their tension reliably over time so that is one more resistance variable eliminated. I hope you are not thinking 'phew'. Let's recap on what we've got to go on so far:

- Bike with crank length and saddle same as road bike. Full range of gears and rear wheel computer.
- Simple fold-out turbo trainer with good monitoring brackets, magnetic resistance and spring loaded.

At this point in time do not rush out and get a turbo bike until you have gone to Chapter 3 on bike set-up since it might transpire that you need different crank length from what you are using right now and there is no point incurring the extra expense and wastage on this issue. In my experience this issue particularly affects women riders, for the simple reason that the industry tends to fob off smaller riders with non-proportioned equipment simply because shorter cranks and handlebars are counted as non-standard and cost more to the manufacturer.

The turbo unit is a different matter. Either you have a magnetic unit already or you are going to buy one. I'll give you the bad news first – the standard unit is or will not be up to scratch for my training plan in most cases as it

comes. The good news is that with a bit of work it will be up to scratch. It needs to be adapted in two or three ways and if you are not technical or mechanically minded, don't worry since a good independent bike shop with a decent mechanic can do the work for you.

> ## personally speaking if I work that hard for improvement, I want to know for *sure* that is my *actual* improvement

The first thing is that if the unit has a fan attachment as well as a mag unit then the fan has to be removed for the reason stated earlier. Even if the fan is small and seems to be part of a cooling mechanism, don't be fooled into thinking it won't matter. It will. Even if it only makes 5 per cent of resistance then at 10 per cent variance for air pressure that equals 0.5 per cent inaccuracy – the amount of difference you might want to be sure to have improved in one ride. Personally speaking if I work that hard for improvement, I want to know for *sure* that is my *actual* improvement as an athlete. Basically I need to know that if the computer says I have improved 0.5 per cent, then that is actually my gain physically and not some other factor.

The other main issue is the cable control that loosens or tightens the resistance; this source of inaccuracy must also be eliminated. Do not forget that you will be using the gears on your bike to make it easier or harder. I have de-commercialised and made accurate several of these machines over the years and here are my preferred choices. The best option to set your machine for life is to remove the side panel and clamp the adjustment device with a piece of gear cable that comes with it or some sort of permanent stop that means the resistance is set solid for life. If you are lucky enough to find a magnetic unit with no cable adjust then the problem is solved. If you do this right and have it set firmly to nearly the maximum resistance so that you are using a middle gear for a prolonged effort and lower gears for warming up, then you have extra gears for improved fitness and you never need think about it again – you're good to go.

I admit that this gold standard in set-piece accurate hardware does take a bit of fiddling and technical knowledge – not rocket science but still bike mechanic level input. If you want it enough and believe in what I am trying to achieve for you in this book, you will find someone who can help you in this. Don't worry though, since the second option is almost as good. If you take the cable adjust lever and simply set the machine to the hardest setting

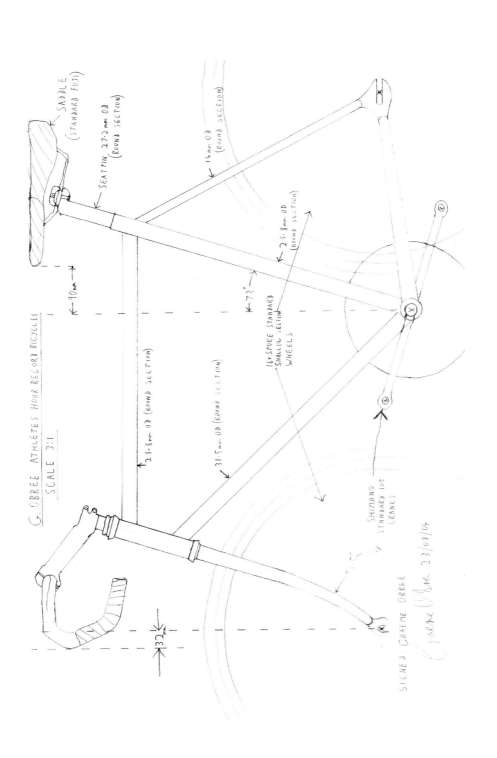

G. OBREE ATHLETES HOUR RECORD BICYCLE!

SCALE 3:1

SADDLE
(STANDARD FUJI)

SEATPIN 27·2mm OD
(ROUND SECTION)

14mm OD
(ROUND SECTION)

23·8mm OD
(ROUND SECTION)

←73°

16T SPOKE STANDARD
SHALLOW SECTION
WHEELS

←90mm→

23·8mm OD (ROUND SECTION)

31·5mm OD (ROUND SECTION)

SHIMANO
STANDARD 105
CRANKS

32mm

SIGNED GRAEME OBREE

Graeme Obree 23/03/04

you can then roll the cable (including the control lever) up into a coil about the width of a small football – no tighter since the tight wind loosens the machine again. Simply tape and tie the coil onto the same leg of the machine as the magnetic unit. Make sure it cannot move in relation to the unit but leave enough loose cable for spring loading movement. There is an even easier option still which is sometimes possible. If you put a standard bike on your mag turbo, put it in the hardest setting and if that is usable to warm up and have a training setting *and* the cable at the mag unit end has a tiny bit of play or movement – in other words the adjustment inside the unit has reached its end point – cut the entire cable off with a pair of pliers.

The whole process is a nuisance and inconvenient and it would be understandable if you just bypassed it but the importance of accuracy cannot be overstated. Fully accurate, single-setting machines may be available commercially and this may not be necessary. Look on the bright side though – once you have done this or obtained a suitable machine you will have an amazing tool of self-improvement that only those obsessively dedicated to their sport and following this instruction will have. It seems a lot, but in reality this can be done in an afternoon. There are magnetic resistance machines with no cable control already and the market develops quickly. If you come across one and you are convinced by the manufacturer's long-term accuracy statistics then this could solve all the hassle.

There is just one more thing to be done to your turbo to make it conform to the 'Obree Way' of training. This is optional but advisable. Every commercial turbo comes with a fly-wheel on the opposite side from the magnetic unit. I ask you to remove it or have your local shop remove it for you. It may be worth telling them that it is most likely fitted using a 'left hand thread'. The reason for this is that pedalling is as complicated as a swimming stroke and certainly not an up and down affair. Removing the fly-wheel will help train an all round more efficient stroke. I explain all in the section about pedalling, but for now, trust me, and get rid of it!

GIven the current fashion for marketing ever more complicated turbo trainers it may require some diligent shopping to locate the model with the simple features I decribe. An ideal solution would be that a manufacturer provides a single setting resistance trainer I have described, with the feature of lateral movement – a function that would be more useful than any other gimmick on the market today, and signs are that the market will respond to this need. It also might be that you have looked at crank or hub power measuring units already or it might be the case that when enquiring about turbo trainers someone might try to talk you into investing in this. My honest opinion on this type of equipment is that not only is it of no real use in real-time training, it is another distraction from the path of true self-improvement. I have the same opinion of computers for road use and heart-rate monitors, but for one exception. The heart-rate monitor can be useful when going out on a proper recovery ride to not let team-mates force you to ruin your recovery by going too fast. The reason is simply that these appliances complicate the job of training on the road, and they are hard to use as instant feedback training aids in that training environment. I'm not a fan of analogies but these devices are equivalent to a car speedometer that tells you what speeds you did once you have stopped – interesting, but useless. Besides, once you have read the chapters on breathing and pedalling, you will have enough to think about on a ride without adding fundamentally useless data.

One other important factor if we are going to be businesslike in our new approach is this – where are our permanent business premises? Where exactly is your turbo going to be set up whether it be a permanent set-up or taken down every time? It is important that you can either go straight to a permanent rig or set one up exactly the same every time with the least amount of effort or thought. Pushing yourself to a new level in an aerobic session requires a huge amount of willpower and mental energy so the least amount of thought and effort to set up your rig beforehand has to be a prime goal. A lot of readers will have to consider others in this matter and if, for example, the only suitable place is somewhere in the kitchen then communication and agreement with those others is necessary to avoid friction and ultimately distraction and demotivation towards your training. It is important to secure one spot where you can set up every time and where others can go about their business of cooking or whatever else simply in order that you're training is not compromised by other people's schedules. Partners and family can feel resentful of your ambition, energy and time being expended on sport and not them as it is, so the more accommodating you can be in caring about their free movement and quality of life the better. No matter what though, you do have to be able to secure a permanent exact spot where you will set up every time.

In your permanent spot you will have to have a spot in front of your turbo to place a fan. It can either be a desk fan or one with a stand. Either way it has to be a proper good-sized model for the simple reason that heat build-up is a large impediment to completing a session. Excessive body temperature is a very uncomfortable experience as it is. Also, it restricts your ability to output your maximum effort. A very important point to make in regard to where you set up your rig is that what is good in one season might not be good in another. Most people who have a garage and a partner will end up in, guess where, the garage. A garage in summer is fine but in winter and, more importantly, in spring it can be very cold. Riding in temperatures below 10°C is still useful but not efficient in the scheme of systematic improvement of your aerobic base.

This may seem to contradict what I stated elsewhere in this manual, about heat build-up, but breathing in cold air at a maximum aerobic rate is a route to ill health as much as anything. The main problem is that the lungs do not work efficiently if the temperature is low, and therefore in spring when you want to be seeing effort by effort gains in power, you will struggle in the cold. The solution to this can be twofold. You can agree to train indoors at a set-up spot when it is cold or you can get a fan heater (actually it takes about three to heat a garage and still have ventilation). My advice on this is that if you are stuck in the garage then use three fan heaters but let your partner think there is only one. If you do train indoors, make sure you have ventilation as well as heating. The fact is that the amount of oxygen an athlete consumes in an aerobic effort can deplete a room's-worth quite quickly, and it is important, during cold conditions, for your maximum ride, that you have a good supply of fresh but heated air.

As far as your road training bike is concerned it is important to have a machine that has a similar handlebar position to your race bike and again with a saddle position as close as possible to your race or riding bike. What you really want is a bike that is ready to roll on any type of road and in almost any weather condition and in either night or day. This is the most important bike that you own simply because this is the bike that you ride most often, and it is the bike you will rely on to be ready to go with no fuss or time wasting. If you work and need to do a good road ride during the week, it is vital that you have a machine that is ready to go straight back out the door whatever the weather or daylight conditions. Better still, a bike you can train on directly from your work – with luggage capacity to make that possible.

The luggage capacity issue is actually quite a big one. If you are dividing your time between work, family and friends then no riding opportunity can be ignored. An example of this is when you need to turn your legs over gently to loosen tired muscles in recovery. I would never miss a chance to just ride easy but with other commitments this means setting valuable time aside to achieve just this one task unless you can use your bike to multi-task to do things like getting some shopping in. This, of course, depends on having luggage capacity on at least one of your machines, preferably the main training bike. Most of my cycling friends do not possess such a machine, get the shopping and other run-about jobs in the car and then complain that they don't have enough time to ride! I'm always aware of writing this book for ordinary people and I have to instil the idea that lifestyle change can improve your cycling as well as the impact that cycling has on relationships around about you.

Depending on where you live in the world it would be highly recommended that you have full length mudguards. The most important thing is that when you want and need to train you are not constrained by weather or darkness.

Lights will be a must of course and the choice of wheel and tyre is important as well. Your training bike should have reliable cheaper wheels with full spoking, normally 32 spokes. The choice of tyre is important since the last thing you want in the middle of a good effort is a puncture. Not only does it destroy a good effort but there is the problem of getting cold in the middle of nowhere sorting a puncture that could be avoided. I choose the widest possible tyre that will fit into my bike. These are usually 26mm tyres, and to further reduce the chance of puncture I choose tyres with a puncture resistance. What a lot of cyclists do not realise is that most punctures are not instant but are the result of a piece of debris or glass that works its way through the casing as miles pass by. If you take a look at the outer tyre after each ride or before setting out, you find small flints on the surface that are actively working their way through the rubber and eventually the capcase. You can kill this dead by picking out these specks and the chance of 'instant' puncture will be very much reduced.

With good care, your training bike will be a vehicle of effort you can rely on. I personally, living on the west coast of Scotland, would not feel safe unless I had at least two spare tubes and a patch repair kit. I also carry an emergency kit of tools but if you are not mechanically minded then the fully charged mobile phone has to be your fallback position. If you follow my training bike rules of best tyres and solid industry standard wheels then the chance of being left stranded is quite small. The commercial range of reliable wheels and indeed bikes is better than ever before but be careful not to be mis-sold. A major point in regard to buying a bike that is not only a training device but a means of getting the shopping in is the choice of pedals. You will often see cyclists walking in cycling shoes doing their best imitation of Bambi on ice. The only pedal system that helps you avoid looking like a Disney character when wearing the shoes that go with them is those that allow recessed clips. My favoured type is (Shimano's) SPD.

You need a solid, well-tyred and mudguarded machine. A bike that you can jump onto that will not let you down in the middle of an important road ride. I'll talk in other chapters about what your road rides must be. All you have to know is that your training bike has to be reliable and a machine that you can use for serious effort or for doing a recovery ride to the shops or other family needs.

One of the most important features of your training bike is that it has a wide range of gears. This will be needed in the true path of proper training and proper recovery. This will also be covered in later chapters.

IN BRIEF

The turbo, provided the set-up is meticulous, is like a personalised control experiment and will provide close to 100 per cent accurate data on your performance and allow you to understand and deliver measurable incremental improvement and to assess the effect of your training programme. The training bike needs to be fit for purpose and sound mechanically and as near identical in size to your racing bike within the allowance of your budgetary constraints.

- It is vital that conditions for measuring your performance on the turbo are fixed in order that you can accurately measure and monitor your performance
- This provides you with a personal index of performance that you can compare against all other performances on that turbo set-up
- Magnetic turbo trainers are the most accurate in regard to non-variance in their reaction to atmospheric conditions (air temperature/pressure)
- Think carefully on the location of your turbo set-up, training must be made as convenient as possible for you and others around you
- A good, well-thought-out and maintained training bike is essential with the right support equipment to ensure you can complete your ride whatever the conditions

Bike set-up

There is such a confusing range of bikes and equipment out there that it must be difficult for the average person to know exactly what to buy. There are two things that are constants in the decision-making process and knowing these can help you be confident in your choices. Firstly, the laws of physics don't change, and because the basic design of regulation racing bikes has not changed since the 1890s, the limiting factors are pretty much the same as well and I will get to that in a minute. Secondly, the want of profit is the prime motivating force in the development and sale of expensive bike equipment.

The fact is that a bicycle is as simple a device as can be and although the differences between wheels, frames and components seem quite considerable that is not always the case. Above a certain standard, the performance advantage becomes insignificant and in a lot of cases hardly worth paying the extra money for. In a lot of cases the emphasis has been on weight reduction, which offers a huge selling advantage, to the neglect of aerodynamic efficiency, which is more important most of the time. This trend has been driven by cyclists' own measure of value and quality where the first thing they will do is feel the weight of a bike or component. Try not to fall into this trap.

The first and most important thing when choosing a bike, or if you already own a bike then an upgrade, is quantifying how specific and beneficial it is to you in relation to what events you actually want to do well in. The most important thing in any bike set-up is whether it is morphologically correct (is it the correct fit?). I mentioned before about crank length (9.5 per cent of your height) but available saddle adjustment is important and the size of the frame will alter the height and length and reach of the handlebars.

If you are not sure about what you need by way of bar reach, bar width and crank length then it may be worth the investment in being measured up by a reputable bike-fitting organisation. If you choose this route, ask about for recommendations or solicit feedback through the good online cyclist websites. When it comes to bar width on a standard road position then it is worth bearing in mind that every centimetre of extra width adds considerable aerodynamic drag. A lot of times riders use whatever width of bars they have become accustomed to but on my own bike I have chosen the narrowest available and have turned the brake levers in slightly to reduce the aerodynamic drag on the arms to a minimum.

When you know what you want dimensionally then you have to choose equipment based upon a compromise of weight, aerodynamic profile, reliability and of course price. A famous quote in the bicycle industry is 'light, strong, cheap – choose any two'. Now we know from the laws of physics that aerodynamics plays a major part in the performance of cycling – we have to add this to the mix. For most of us, it is the option of cheap that gets squeezed out in the quest for the other two important qualities.

There is a question of gearing in a performance machine, and now it is possible to have 30 or more gears. Personally I dislike so many gears since it quite often takes several clicks to get the gear I actually want and the more cogs there are on the rear cassette the more clicking you need to do. Also, the chains for 10- and 11-speed cassettes wear out more quickly than 8- or 9-speed, and the adjustment is very sensitive to the slightest knock. Let me pose a question to help you overcome commercial pressure. How many cogs are too many? Fifteen? Forty? And how many would you pare it back to? For me, it's eight or nine. If you must go along with fashion then the important thing is the highest and lowest gears are sufficient for the event you plan to do. I also have to say that as far as time-trial bikes are concerned it is a real benefit in efficiency to have a larger-than-usual front ring. A lot of research was done in the 1990s into chain drive efficiency, and it was found that riding on the 11- and 12-tooth cog was less efficient than having a larger ring and using a larger cog on the rear. This also improves the chainline to cogs that are nearer the middle of the cassette. The largest off-the-shelf chainring is 58 teeth from T.A., but you can buy them any size from specialists, although they are quite expensive.

As far as materials go, carbon fibre seems to have become ubiquitous across most parts of the modern bicycle. This has happened because of the weight advantage in some components and because until now it has been seen as the material to be seen with. The problem in a lot of frame designs is that they tend to be very blobby with some tubes being twice the size of their steel or titanium counterparts. If you can get a carbon-fibre frame that is more aero but not too heavy, then the consideration would be the price and the fact the carbon fibre is very easily damaged by any knocks or bashes. If you crash on it, it can be damaged in a way that is not visible whereas if a

◆

LIGHT
STRONG
CHEAP

◆

- choose any two -

metal frame ain't bent, it ain't damaged. If carbon does fail on you, it does so catastrophically – it will give out instantly and completely. I know people who have lost their front teeth by this very phenomenon.

Titanium is a material that will literally last a lifetime. To be honest the cheaper models are heavier than they need to be, but the dearer models are truly classy. For a standard road bike titanium has the advantage that it will withstand a side-on knock or a large chipping stone that carbon will not, and will also give a more comfortable ride. Steel has the same quality but few builders are able and willing to build bikes light enough to compete with titanium. There are a handful that will though, and if you do go down the bike-fit process, then you will have exact specification for a made-to-measure frame.

One very important issue in any frame or bike that you buy is tyre clearance. A lot of frames leave little clearance for wider tyres, and carbon frames are bad for this in general. It would be easy to believe that a narrower tyre will be faster than a wider one but this is most certainly not the case. The narrower a tyre is then the longer the footprint on the road, and this causes more resistance than a shorter, wider footprint from a wider tyre. Not only this but a wider tyre will puncture less easily and give a smooth ride. The ideal for racing purposes is around 23mm and for sportives a tyre of 25mm or 26mm is an ideal compromise on comfort and speed.

don't rush into buying a bike or kit until you have had time to think on how needed or appropriate it is

There is always the debate about whether to use tubular tyres (glue on) or wired-on with removable inner tubes. If your ambition is centred on racing, the solution is to have both and only use the best tyres (tubular) in important events. If you are a flat line time-triallist, then the slight extra weight of wired-on won't matter and a top quality cover (tyre) will roll as efficiently as a tubular tyre when combined with a light inner tube. For sportives I would never recommend anything other than wired-on. For bunch riding on the road there is a weight saving with tubular tyres that might be worth going for in hilly events, but wired-on are more economic to run since an inner tube can be repaired or replaced so much more easily and cheaply than tubular. Also, spare inner tubes are lighter to carry. Tubular tyres are also dangerous to corner on after being changed on the road since the replacement tyre is rarely stuck on as well as the original, especially when carried out in wet conditions.

When setting up any machine there is always the option of adding a secondary brake lever for one of the brakes. On a time-trial bike it is the rule in some places that the brakes are fitted to the widest part of the handlebars but this is not the best place to have to reach to in readiness of maybe having to brake on a corner. It is faster and smoother to stay on the tri-bars and use a secondary lever that pulls the front brake. It is also safer since if you are in the tri-bar and have to stop suddenly then normally you would have to ride one-handed twice before applying full braking whereas with a secondary lever in the racing position it is much easier. In a team time trial it makes it much safer and easier because you can just touch the lever to drop back a fraction from the wheel you are following.

It is useful on a road bike as well to place the secondary lever on either side of the stem. It does not matter if it pulls the front or rear calliper since its purpose is to lose pace and avoid running up the back of other riders while eating or drinking from a bottle. What does matter is that it is the opposite side of your handlebars. So if you are right-handed and use that hand to eat or drink then the lever would be on the left to lose pace with no panic. If you do elite triathlon and are allowed drafting, a secondary lever on one of the tri-bar arms allows you to ride aero in a group and save energy.

Another point worth mentioning is the practice of having smaller wheels (650c) in triathlon bikes and regular road bikes. It is best to have traditional size (700c) wheels since there is so much more choice of tyres and it is so much easier to upgrade wheels later on. There is lower rolling resistance with them as well. The array of wheels available to purchase is quite bewildering but one thing that is good to take on board is that the front wheel is the most important both aerodynamically and in controlling the bike. I would strongly recommend having a shallow section front wheel at any event where it might be windy. The loss aerodynamically is nowhere near what a lot of manufacturers claim and the loss of rhythm due to front end instability will cost much more in speed anyhow.

Another factor that limits the efficiency of your machine is the condition of your chain. I don't mean how old or worn it is although this needs to be kept on top of, I mean how clean and well oiled it is at the start and during your ride. On wet days and especially during longer rides the oil gets washed out of the chain which leads to a severe loss of power being transferred to the rear wheel from the pedals. A perfectly clean chain can be 97 per cent or 98 per cent efficient but that drops to below 90 per cent or less in the worst conditions. That difference is massive and there are two very good solutions to this. When you consider that this power loss is equivalent to being five or six kilos heavier on a climb then you can see that this is worth taking seriously. This is a win or lose difference.

On a sportive ride there are always feed stops that are opportunities for reoiling your chain using a small bottle of oil but in a race situation it is different. Unless you rig up a reoiling device of your own making, then the only real option is to fit a Scotoiler. This is a device that operates from a squeezy squid mounted on your handlebars and actually uses a surfactant (a soup-like emulsion) that needs to be fed regularly to the chain. This is actually more efficient than oil from the start. The only drawback is the real hassle of fitting a Scotoiler and the ugliness of tubes running along your bike, the main reason that it never became the commercial success it should have. Again, if you are not technically minded, get your bike shop to fit it for you.

In short, don't rush into buying a bike or kit until you have had time to think on how needed or appropriate it is. Always be willing to play about with position and be mindful of the fact that it is very easy to get used to something that is not quite right, especially crank length.

IN BRIEF

Bike set-up can be the difference between success and failure in your chosen discipline. Pay attention to every detail – understanding the biomechanical relationship between you and your bike is essential to ensuring you achieve the correct set-up.

- Think of your bike specifically in relation to the events you wish to do well in
- Experiment with your position and don't be afraid to experiment with your equipment – what is right for one person is not necessarily right for another

04

The turbo session

The turbo session is the key component of systematic improvement, provided you can be sure of your machines accuracy as I described earlier in the book. Knowing that sustained power output is the ultimate measure and making of the cyclist whatever your discipline, combined by absolute confidence in the figures you are producing, is the key to unlocking the resolve to complete this training exercise.

The session on the turbo, although it is relatively short in time spent riding, is critical to overall improvement. This is a session where psychology and physiological preparation play a larger part in the success than the physical state, provided proper recovery has been followed. This is why it is so important that the environment that you create for this effort is as free of disruption/distraction as possible. It is not necessary or even possible most of the time to create a hermetically sealed mini-universe of perfect isolation. I have to make it clear that the only distraction that really matters is another human trying to gain your attention during the focus zone and the ride itself.

The key to this is communication from you about how it is not possible to make any contact – especially eye contact – at any time, not even to confirm a yes or no answer to a question. Doing the hoovering or doing the dishes is fine so long as it is clear that normal social norms or acknowledgement are suspended for that time. Part of this battle is within yourself to abrogate the ingrained social norms of looking at someone or even just raising an eyebrow. So long as you make it clear that this is a relatively short training session and by explaining that when it gets really tough a distraction is a good excuse or a valid reason to chuck it. Remember, if you have ditched ambling useless rides with your club-mates and spend more time at home, then not only will you be in better shape for it, you will get better support for this one crucial ride.

Ideally, though, a place out of the home environment is the better option. For a long time in my career I used to use a cleaned out coal-cupboard the size of a small toilet cubicle and I know many riders who use old garden sheds. Assuming things are set up as I described in Chapter 2, the important thing is now the process and getting started.

Initially what you have is a bike with a computer but no idea how hard you should ride. If, for example, you choose to use the 20-minute or 30-minute session options, then all you can do at the start is set off at what feels like a reasonable effort. If perhaps at half distance you realise you can ride harder, then raise the pace but remember all of this is about riding at the same speed and not being erratic – raise the pace, then stick rigidly to that speed. In the end you will have the very first results to put into you turbo-training log. It will take three or four rides to really get a grip on the pace that really challenges you.

As you progress with your rides it is good to bring in more ritual and build-up, not only because it is a good way to focus the mind, but also the rides will be getting more difficult and a prepared and focused mind is less likely to allow a 'giving up' situation. Remember that the body cannot do anything without the mind making it, so part of every turbo session is about strengthening the resolve of the mind. A strengthened mind is an asset that will stand you in good stead in all aspects of cycling.

In the real world after a day at work and then coming home and spending time with partners or family, your mind is not in that zone. Few individuals possess the ability to switch into a new zone instantly, leaving the previous domestic zone behind completely. Few of us have no worries or concerns or thoughts about what we have to do tomorrow. To undertake a session that not only reaches our physical limit but exceeds it a little fraction requires a mind that is completely in that zone and only that zone.

So here is what you have to do. Tell those you are abandoning that you will be out of circulation for an hour, barring genuine emergencies. You go to your machine, recheck the tyre pressure as I said earlier, check the fan in front of you is plugged in and facing at a good angle. Make sure the temperature is appropriate – a bit of forward practice in all of this is good practice. So you end up on your machine and warming up. I like to have extra layers of clothing on top and peel them off as I heat up from the effort. Ideally you will have a water bottle and Olbas oil (decongestant) within easy reach. If you are lucky enough to be outside and away from distraction, then you will also have an old jug to do one last pee before you start. Going back to the domestic residence can completely destroy the zone with the added danger of, for example, your partner saying, 'Johnny isn't doing his homework – you need to have a quick word with him'. Non-athletic types cannot possibly understand no matter how much explanation you give so best-policy preparation is not to need to go back inside!

— CREATING —

• a mini •

UNIVERSE

You get the picture already that this is about being in the *zone*. At the start you are just getting figures and finding your limit, but when it comes to stretching that limit it requires a new and intensely focused build-up. A gentle warm-up at the beginning is a good start. When you start on your machine it is essential to focus on the effort you are going to undertake. Focus on the moment you will finish and how good you will feel at that point when you get to write in your log that you just did your personal best and what it means in the real world in terms of personal improvement. A good warm-up could last as long as 30 minutes and during that time you will want to go incrementally harder but never reaching anywhere near the pace you will be holding during the actual session. You want to be sipping water and toward the approach of going for it you want to have at least one last pee and put a tiny drop of Olbus Oil on the end of one finger and apply to both nostrils. This helps open the airways and at least gives the physiological benefit of a sense of readiness.

A very good idea is to set an exact moment to start, at which point you get up to speed on the gear you choose and reset the computer so that when you stop it at the end of your session, you will have distance and average speed. Set the computer to speed and in km/hr since you will need to look at this constantly during the session. The main point of the long warm-up is that you get in the *zone* where you are focused on nothing but the output of this one ride.

An important point to clarify is what to eat beforehand. If, as most people have to, you do this session after work, then you have to put off dinner till after the session. During the session almost hungry is the best way and nibbling on something light like banana or crackers to stave off the feeling of real hunger is the way to go. Hydration is also important and it is worth noting that rehydration actually takes quite a while, and if you are working and commuting then it is important to forward plan and take water with you. A thing to keep in mind is that a feeling of tiredness is normal, but usually this is in reality mental tiredness and not physical since few of us output huge numbers of calories at work in this day and age in Western economies. Knowing this will allow us to combat it and, let's be honest, as human beings we tend to make excuses not to do things. The truth is after the warm-up and the ride itself you know you will feel better than you would if you bailed out and just couched it. Make a point of reminding yourself of this after each session to reinforce the sense of benefit.

The warm-up period is the most important part of the process since being in the right frame of mind to start your effort is the biggest factor in not giving up. It is a good thing to focus on the importance of completing this ride and the fact that these minutes ahead of you determine totally how good you will make yourself as a cyclist. Another factor to concentrate on is what you achieved in your previous ride and bearing in mind that you are shooting out for achievable and fractional improvement, then you can give yourself the confidence of knowledge that this is fully achievable.

To properly explain this I have to describe the process of systematic improvement. From my own experience it is only possible to improve by 1km/hr at the start of the turbo programme. After a few rides the realistic improvement is 1km/hr for part of the ride since 1km/hr is equal to in excess of 2 per cent – neither possible nor sustainable at the point of actual improvement. For example, if I had achieved 47km/hr for 20 minutes and been completely on my limit physically and mentally at the end part of this effort, then the next session I would line up is 47km/hr for 15 minutes and five minutes at 48km/hr. The point is that using a series of small increments means that you can have absolute confidence that you can do at least three quarters of the ride – because you did it last week! The only difference is the five minutes at the higher rate. What you have to do is not use excessive mental energy on the first part of the ride; you know you can do this part!

In the warm-up, think about the part that will challenge you and where you are most likely to give up. I told you earlier about how you reach your immediate ability and then stretch it. That lasts five minutes. That five minutes is the most important of your entire training week and the best way to approach the rest of the ride is to concentrate on rhythm, breathing and good pedal action. Make a conscious decision that you will not unleash your determination and mental energy until that vital point where you are breaking new ground.

In my experience the most dangerous time is when it seems like so long yet to ride and you feel at the end of your tolerance already. In a 20 minute ride it happens at about 12 or 13 minutes. In a 30 minute ride it normally occurs about 17 or 18 minutes. The way to counter it is to concentrate absolutely on rhythm and think only about getting to the 15 or 20 minute mark. Once you are there, then it seems like the home run and doable. I have caved in at these times and felt really bad about it, only because within a minute I realise I could have gone on. If this happens to you, all you can do is go back the next day or the day after and make good. This is the absolute key session of improvement and you must do this before moving on to the next ride.

A lot of turbo-training riding is tied up with distraction and there are loads of gimmicks and programmes like video and virtual riding. The reason I dismiss them is that there is enough to think about during the ride with breathing and pedalling, but more than anything the real-time feedback about how hard you must ride is not specific enough. Not only that but you cannot be sure that the machine is accurate enough to be sure of that 0.5 per cent improvement. Having said that, I do appreciate that doing a session like I describe is very hard and some distraction is welcome if it does not impinge on the quality of the effort. Music can be the answer to a lot of boredom and can help in the focus and rhythm of the ride. In my experience music with discernible words in your native language can be a negative distraction in that your mind follows the words to come and you lose concentration on the complicated job of breathing, pedalling and holding perfect pace. The best music choice I developed over the years is ethnic music where there is a strong rhythm but because I cannot understand the words there is no distraction, yet the upbeat tempo helps the minutes pass by.

I have to come to the point of what really matters – the point where you are going to improve yourself as a cyclist, the point where you have reached your personal limit of your current physical condition and you are now 'stretching the envelope'. This stretching is uncomfortable and difficult, and there is no way of getting round this fact. You have to think about this point in the ride as the part that will improve you and the first three-quarters as the effort needed to bring you to this point where you can harvest the benefits. If you think of it this way, then you weigh up all the importance on that part of the ride. If you have it clear in your mind that if you cave in at this point, the entire effort will be wasted – this focuses the resolve.

> ## the point where no further improvement can be made is actually further than we think it is simply because we can always do more than we think we can, but a plateau will be reached sooner or later

There comes a point where ultimately it comes down to you, your power and resolve. The truth is that this clinical form of training is debilitating and difficult to sustain mentally in the long term. The vast majority of riders give up on it after a bit in favour of interval training or just riding on the road. It is also a truth that without this forced improvement in aerobic power then it is almost impossible for a rider to reach their true personal potential. If you fall into this category, then perhaps you ought to question how much time and money you should continue to invest in your sport. Alternatively, you could reappraise the goals you have in mind and the events you have lined up for the simple reason that you clearly won't be competing at your true potential. If it is the case that you just don't want to endure this constant stretching process, then this could be an ideal point in time to consider reducing your expense and commitment and perhaps moving to a more

BREAKING

- *new* -

GROUND

leisure-centred approach. You could even make more time for other hobbies or family and friends.

Assuming you are finishing your sessions, you will start to get quite a body of information and it is useful to put race results and comments about how you felt in your log with dates as well as a description of the conditions. This is really useful later on when you look back against what you did on the turbo and what your form was like in the real world. You could log your heart-rate in the last minute if you wanted to and this certainly lets you know that you were in the red zone, but ultimately the only information that actually matters is average speed.

> ## there will be times when it's the warmth of summer and beautiful sunshine but the effort on the static bike is the most important thing

Clearly there has to be a cut-off point where no further improvement can be made. The point is actually further than we think it is simply because we can always do more than we think we can, but a plateau will be reached sooner or later. This is a good thing since it means you have worked to get close to your physical limit and at this point all you can do is move to micro-improvements. At some point it also becomes the off-season, and it isn't good to continue at the edge of your ability, either physically or mentally. There is a level of output that you really don't want to fall below, and a minimum standard of no more than 6 or 8 per cent of your peak velocity has to be your standard, even in mid-winter. The old idea of just letting it all go at the end of the season is not the best policy – as far as form goes, it is much easier to maintain it, albeit with a planned step back in the off-season, then regaining full output again.

As far as in-season riding is concerned then this is the most important time to be putting in turbo efforts. There will be times when it's the warmth of summer and beautiful sunshine but the effort on the static bike is the most important thing. It is easy to be tempted to do a road ride instead but there is nothing to stop you going on an easy road ride after, and since you will have pushed your limit already then a gentle ride with family or partner would be beneficial to relationship harmony as well.

One last tip is that if you have a spring-loaded roller on a permanent set-up then it will leave an indentation on the tyre which will cause a very annoying bumping as the wheel turns. The simple solution is to slip a flat object, like a butter knife, between the roller and the tyre at the end of each ride.

IN BRIEF

The turbo session is about preparation, visualisation, goal setting and pushing your athletic output to a higher level.

- Ensure the environment is right for your turbo session
- Goal setting and visualisation are vital to allow you to 'stretch the envelope'
- Think about the rhythm of the cycle action and the role music can play
- Above all, don't give up and revert to a less demanding option; focus and target on your end goal

05

Training

Since the purpose of training is to stimulate physiological adaptation then it is important to look at the most effective means of causing that to happen. The most important physical attribute to develop is speed and close behind it is the ability to sustain speed for a prolonged period. The best way to achieve this is to use different intensities of effort and pedalling rates for different distances in order to maximise speed, strength and endurance.

> competing almost every weekend can actually be counterproductive in the process of long-term systematic improvement

The most important effort in the training cycle is the aerobic workout on the turbo trainer. This has to be done from a position of total recovery and really this has to be considered the first ride in the cycle. I will go into more detail on this key effort in the next chapter but it fundamentally requires the greatest mental and physical input of any of the subsequent rides. Its importance is such that failure to improve on the first ride undermines the ability to improve overall. The most important thing to be said about this is that complete recovery and physical freshness are vital when it is undertaken.

Obviously I am aware that a lot of readers will have a full racing programme lined up that involves competing almost every weekend. This can actually be counterproductive in the process of long-term systematic improvement. Firstly because this ties the athlete to a schedule that requires them to be relatively fresh in order to do a reasonable ride and as such means they are frequently having to taper back their training or reduce the vital training sessions, which are needed in order to develop enhanced performance. Secondly, if that ride is a short or medium distance time trial then there is no feedback control to know that real improvement has been forced. Only after the event does the rider know how they performed and with weather and course variability, real improvement is impossible to ascertain. Nonetheless, in the circumstance it may be necessary to count a time trial as a substitute for a measured turbo effort. If the race is longer, then a measured turbo session can be done later in the week – usually on at least Wednesday to allow total recovery. That allows one ride on Thursday or Friday before the race or not at all if the race is on Saturday. So you see, the seven-day cycle is not ideal and the best thing to be honest is not to race every weekend.

Assuming that you are only targeting important events and only riding every other weekend then this allows you to concentrate on the programme of training for sustained improvement. The next important ride is the ride on the road for an hour or so, which you should treat like a time trial. This ride could be a 25-mile time trial that you want to ride, but it will be compromised by the previous turbo effort, bearing in mind that despite the intensity of that effort it is possible to perform almost at your best within a couple of days since it causes more strain on the aerobic system than the muscles themselves. Also, absolute recovery is not essential before undertaking this ride. This is the length of ride that stresses both the aerobic and muscular systems pretty much equally. I also have to make it clear that this ride in the process is optional depending upon what your event is and how long it lasts.

> **other riders will want to talk to you on a two-hour ride, but the truth is if you can chat then you are wasting your time and opportunity to improve**

The next and totally essential ride is what I call the glycogen ride. This has to be done on the road and lasts between 1 hour 30 minutes and 2 hours 20 minutes, depending on your physical condition at that time. I call this the glycogen ride since I usually undertake this after a reasonable period of recovery and have only a modest intake of food beforehand. I have to explain that glycogen is what your muscles actually run on and copious amounts of food will only make you feel bunged up and make zero difference to your energy output. One of the reasons to do a ride of this length is to deplete

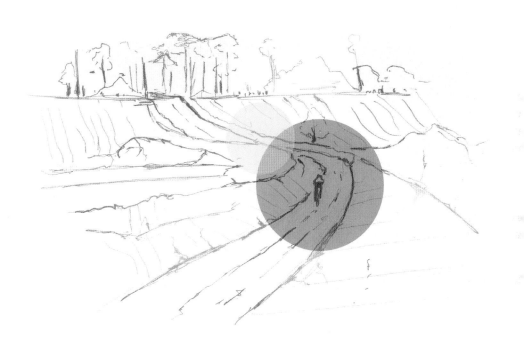

the glycogen and train the body to both use glycogen and store it more efficiently. It is stored in the muscles and in the liver. The muscle of a trained aerobic athlete has only 30–40 per cent of its mass consisting of muscle fibres. The large majority of mass is the blood supply and energy system so it makes sense to train this part as well.

There are certain parameters to this ride that are important to state. This is the ride where you will need to go hard enough from the start till near the finish (the last two miles in a lower gear is good for recovery) that you could not chat easily with a colleague. This is a ride where you need to be gripping on for the last 20 minutes to maintain your pace and not collapse to almost nothing. You would expect to struggle to deal with your bike and make it up a flight of stairs at the end of your ride.

I say this to define the level of effort. I also have to say that I have rarely found it possible to achieve the purpose and aims of this ride while in the company of any other rider. Fundamentally other riders want to talk to you on a two-hour ride, but the truth is if you can chat then you are wasting your time *and* opportunity to improve. As an aside, I can also say that the power of the mobile phone means that inevitably you will be stood on the side of the road while your 'training partner' takes an 'essential' call. Neither option good. This ride is too important to risk someone else messing it up. I usually ride alone; if others come along, make it clear that there is very little talking to be done and if you get dropped, then it is goodbye. To be the best that you can be, there has to be a time where you make a clear distinction between social and serious riding. For me the distinction was clear: training is too important to be distracted or held back and social riding is often too fast for recovery. The other issue is that during this ride where you concentrate on the pedal and breathing technique any distraction is less than helpful.

What I recommend is working out on a circuit that takes the time you want to ride for. I have several circuits in order to avoid boredom, but I have also worked out 'bolt-ons' where I can add a few miles to an original circuit as I am building up the 'food-free' distance I can cover. It is really important to know in your head *exactly* where you will ride before you leave. I have made the mistake of indecision during a ride and not making the most of it. Even I can be lazy at heart and a decision made during a ride usually results in taking the shorter and easier route.

It is important to point out the necessity for water during a ride: I always make sure I have two bottles. I also always carry a couple of bananas, primarily for the security of knowledge that I have food but also in case of mechanical failure. In most cases I come back with both bananas, and mechanicals are rare since I ride alone and can ride my proper training bike. Expect to arrive completely ready to devour food because, after all, that is part of the remit of the exercise. A word of advice is to prepare some

THINK

to yourself

- see me on race day -

healthy food to consume on your return home since otherwise in the throes of hunger and exhaustion it is a natural instinct to seek out the quickest gobful of choice biscuits or whatever.

My preferred food is sardines on toast with side servings of broccoli and carrots. I prepare this before leaving since the effort of mashing up the sardines can seem like a mammoth task if I do the ride as I described. It may not seem appetising on departure but on return it appears to be a culinary delight! The secret is to put a bit of tomato sauce in the mix. This gives the perfect balance of carbohydrate, protein, vitamins and essential oils such as omega-3. There are other choices, of course, and I will talk about them in Chapter 12. The important thing to know is that at that moment you return, soaked in sweat and needing a shower, you have the perfect recovery meal ready to feed a depleted and hungry body. There are loads of post-ride commercial mixtures available, but none that I have seen can match the nutritional content of this meal. Remember the human body is designed to chew and digest *real* food, and chewing and forming small balls of food is a very important part of the digestive process that commercial drinks disregard. Be cynical; think it through for yourself, there is no profit in telling you that sardines, toast and veggies is one of the best meals you can eat.

There is another training aspect that can be encapsulated in this ride. Absolute muscular strength is clearly an important part of being able to produce the maximum power output when required during a competitive event. Standard gym work is popular among many top riders but I have never allowed myself to be drawn down this path for two reasons. Firstly, a lot of gym work, particularly on fixed-rig equipment, will not strengthen the cycling muscles in a cycling-specific way because this equipment is geared towards strengthening one specific muscle group at a time and not necessarily to the exact stroke or usage for cycling. Secondly, it takes time and travel to go to the gym, and if you have a family and work commitments like many do, then this eats into any free time that could be used to train more effectively or spend valuable time with our families and friends.

This ride is so important that it serves several functions in a couple of hours. Firstly it is a serious ride that trains the aerobic system and muscle groups. It also serves as an opportunity to train the motor circuits to do breathe and pedal control as more of an automatic response. It conditions the glycogen system to store and utilise the glycogen more efficiently. But there is one last aspect as I mentioned earlier: when it comes to muscular strength, there is no better way to improve the strength of the specific contraction (remember, muscles contract) than to perform an overload exercise in the actual range of movement needed for the sport in question. In other words, stress the muscles during the pedal cycle.

What you need to do to make this a complete session in every aspect is to use a hill or gradient on your circuit to grind out a huge gear that you can barely turn over without stalling. You only need to do this once or twice on your circuit to promote extra growth of muscle fibres. It is important to say that this should be done in the sitting position while trying to maintain a good pedalling stroke, thus stressing all the muscle groups in one go.

It has to be said that at the end of this ride you ought to be physically exhausted as well as hungry. All of this coupled with the proper nutrition will instruct the body to change physiologically to the specific adaptation you require to be as good a cyclist as you can be. The following days will see you diminished and tired and this is the time that good nutrition and rest is vital – and not neglecting the stretching routine that I illustrate in the chapter on stretching! As I mentioned earlier, it depends upon your event whether you do a further ride of even greater distance. If for example you do road rides of four hours or more, you may want to do a ride of that length to end your cycle of training. If so, this is a good time to get involved with other riders especially ones that like to have a go now and then as that simulates race conditions with changes of pace.

I have to be clear that if you train your glycogen system in this way then the nutrient uptake system is also trained so it is not necessary to do long rides at the end of each training cycle. If long events are your thing, then it still holds that the turbo session and glycogen ride are the most important elements of your training, but doing a long ride and taking energy from food on the ride will also help train the endurance aspect of your event. I will speak about energy and food in Chapter 12. It may be that you specialise in track events, and in that case it still holds that you follow the incremental distance format and more importantly use the turbo and glycogen ride cycle. In that case you should start the cycle with the distance of your event. For example, when I did pursuit, which is 4km, I would start my training cycle with a 4km effort, move onto the turbo aerobic then a two-hour ride, but of course not do a long ride. It is important to repeat that complete recovery is essential in order to gain improvement in the accurately measured turbo session. To assure some readers, I have to say that on occasion I would take four or even five days to recover from the two-hour session. Of course, I would ride about but my legs would be so jaded that I could not even go on an easy ride with club riders. It is also important to stress that riding with tired legs but going fast enough to hurt is injurious to recovery, and to be honest most club riders don't understand this very important fact. I am not a fan of heart rate monitors but I do find them useful in recovery. If you say you cannot go above 100bpm because you are on a recovery ride, then there is no pride lost if you get dropped. Trust me, I have been dropped by rank amateurs on mountain bikes in recovery. It does not mean you are weak – it means you did it right! Think to yourself: see me on race day!

IN BRIEF

The most important effort in the training cycle is the aerobic workout on the turbo trainer combined with longer rides to improve glycogen storage and usage as well as improving strength. Good rest is vital to allow the body to recover fully between efforts.

- Think and classify your training efforts from small to large
- Most important are the turbo ride and the glycogen ride
- Assess your strengths and weaknesses and target training to combat weakness and consolidate strengths

06

Psychology of preparation

A thought is like a thing. Everything we have and do begins as a thought. The bike you ride and the fact that you ride that bike started with a thought. The entirety of psychology is about what we think and about how we choose to act on those thoughts. We can generally choose what kind of thoughts we have, either positive or negative, and we can choose our actions based on those thoughts. We need not be controlled by our thoughts. We can take control of our thoughts and how we are affected by them. If we gather up our positive thoughts and motives into one bundle, we could call it 'passion'.

Passion is a sentiment that is more usually spoken about in the arts than the world of sport. It gets swept aside in the swirl of real and tangible things like training plans and equipment choice, etc. These are real actual things indeed but so too are thoughts and emotions and attitudes. Passion, the desire to immerse yourself in the field of endeavour that you love, is the foremost and most positive driving force of all.

> I love the sport that I do for myself and I totally want to do it the best that I can

Every single person who competes on a bicycle is passionate about this sport. You spend a good part of your income to do this as well as a huge amount of time and energy. Then there are the sacrifices, like things that you won't eat and the social functions you miss in order to be at your best. If that is not passionate about the sport then what is it? It is nothing other than passion, and if you struggle to place yourself in the world of the passionate, then it is not because you don't belong there. It is because you have been swept along in the world of the physical act of doing. It may be you have never stopped to consider why you do it and how much it means to you. It may be that you have forgotten how passionate you are, through the passage of time. Either way, the desire within you to do this sport is an energy and a positive force so long as you are in touch with it at a conscious level.

While you are reading this your thinking self has no choice but to be focused on why you want to do this as well as how much you want to do this. How much you want to do anything is a matter of choice, and if you accept that this is the first and by far the most important thing that you do for yourself, then the answer is clear. Let me encourage you to be selfish for the moment and set aside family, friends, work and other commitments and think just about you. The question now has to be whether you do your sport because you kind of want to or because you passionately love it and this is the absolute most important thing that you do for yourself. The only answer is that you totally want to do this because you can choose your attitude. From this moment there really only can be one attitude to the sport you love. If it is the case that you can only master indifference then you have to ask yourself whether the sacrifices you make are worth it and whether you ought to go and do something else. I have told you about passion and about how we can choose our attitude. Please take a moment and assess your commitment to a more productive and accurate attitude: I love the sport that I do for myself and I totally want to do it the best that I can.

I wrote earlier about having a choice of thoughts and attitude. This holds true in the issue of thinking positively or negatively in regard to how we are about to perform in an upcoming event. A negative attitude to what we think the end result will be in an event is not an accurate assessment of our true potential. It may be that predictions of substandard results have proven to be accurate in the past. This accuracy of prediction only serves to reinforce the negative thought patterns and it can become an entrenched attitude that is very hard to break out of. At times when a better-than-expected result occurs (compared to the pessimistic prediction), this also reinforces a negative cycle since the feeling of success is based on low expectation from the start.

The route out of a negative thought pattern or to avoid negative thoughts creeping in is to analyse and understand the cause and effect of it. It is easy to believe that the prediction of a poor result and then that result taking place is simply a case of honest assessment of the inevitable.

This is not true! No result is inevitable. If we believe that we have some control over our results by the way we think about the possible outcome beforehand, then we can use our minds to make that result better than it would have been. The first most important thought in the step towards banishing negativity is that we have absolute control over our performance by the way we think before and during an event.

the simple fact of believing that the power of thought will make a difference has already made you a better rider

Obviously the power of thought will not enable you to do more than your physical capability at that time. Few of us, though, ever output our absolute potential in an event no matter how hard we think we are trying and the difference that positive thinking makes is how close to that potential we can get before our mind tells us we can do no more. This phenomenon is most striking in survivors of shipwrecks and similar disasters. Some people have survived the most extreme conditions where others perish sometimes driven by the sheer force of personality, the power of the mind of the survivors. If you believe this is true of survival, you *must* believe it is true of sport. The simple fact of believing that the power of thought will make a difference has already made you a better rider.

The other thought that you must accept into your direct thinking process in the battle against negativity is similar to the first. When you accept that your mind can work for you or against you then you have to accept the logical conclusion. If no result is predetermined or inevitable, then it is clear that negative thoughts about the result are very much self-fulfilling prophecies – you think you will perform badly so you *do* perform badly.

Besides, when you consider that cycling is what you do for yourself as your pastime and sport, then it is something you ought to gain from in a positive sense and ultimately pleasure from. Negative thoughts also permeate into other aspects of your life and can affect your general demeanour as a person and your outlook on other aspects of life.

Positive thinking is not an instant easy alternative to suddenly switch to even if you accept everything I stated already. If negative thinking has been a pattern, it takes time and effort to break the habit. The best way to combat a bad thought process is to counter it every time with what realistically could be your best possible result. A lot of negative thinking is also centred on things that actually you have no control over at all – for example, getting a puncture or another competitor performing better than expected. What you must do is prepare as best you can for any obvious eventualities and then actively refuse to think about them. This is sometimes not easy but a good technique is replacing those thoughts with positive ones about things that you can control like how long you want to warm up for or where you want to make your best effort.

We have control over performance by the way we think.

COUNTERING NEGATIVITY

- No result is inevitable and negative thinking will help make a poor performance a reality
- Counter negative projections with positive thoughts about how good the result might be
- Don't dwell on possibilities that are out of your control; replace these thoughts with positive outcomes from things you can control

Another aspect of thinking in a positive manner is having confidence in your ability either now or in the future in regard to what you are capable of. This is subtly different from thinking positively in that confidence involves believing that you are capable of the result you have in mind. This is the self-belief that, if not right now then some day, with continued progression and a positive attitude, you will be capable of your ultimate goal.

It quite often gets confused with arrogance, and it is easy to understand why when you consider that both attitudes are closely related. Arrogant people achieve more than unconfident and negative people, and super-confidence is also not taken as endearing at a social level. The important difference is that confidence is an assumption of ability based on reality and acceptance that hard work and disappointments lie in the path to it. Arrogance is assuming ability on the unrealistic basis of ego.

There is sometimes a dichotomy between the expressed attitude that makes us fit well into a cooperative society, in which most of us live, and the attitude that drives us to our best results. Basically, there are two issues I must address before I go on. One is the effect that society's like of humbleness and self-depreciation has on us as athletes who need to be positive and confident. The other is the effect on us socially if we big ourselves up and sound overconfident. The solution is to separate both sides of your life and only do humble (and therefore more popular) in a social context and never put down your prospects in your sport. If you do have a conversation about your upcoming event of sport in general, then say something like 'I'll give it my best shot' or something equally neutral.

A

thought

is like a

THING.

It is worth bearing in mind as well that anything that affects your life in general will also affect your sport. The two sides can never be totally separated. The general positivity of a person can go up or down depending on how much positive or negativity they allow into their lives. If putting yourself down is a social habit, then the price of it is going to be a lower level of general positivity that ultimately affects your positive thinking about your sport. So check yourself if you find yourself doing this.

The confidence to achieve a level of performance you achieved before is a good base to start from. If you know what you can do already, that's great, but either way you need to be goal setting. It is not easy to give specific advice in general terms but a long-term goal has to have some element of ambition. A good policy is to look at a rider who is performing better than you in your social/age category and ask yourself what prevents you becoming as good or better. It is sometimes possible to put the differences into percentages and the reason I banged on about accuracy of your turbo trainer set-up in the previous chapter being so important is that if your turbo said you improved 5 per cent, then you can be sure of it. Knowing you have genuinely improved is so important because that gives you confidence and makes it easier to think positively.

POSITIVE THINKING
- Believe in your potential and have confidence that you *can* do it
- Try not to put yourself down in general and never in a sporting sense
- Set ambitious but realistic goals

OK, so you have been thinking positively about your event and you're positive about your ability and longer-term goal but it's first thing in the morning – it might even be raining. You might even get to the event and find yourself in a conversation with other competitors who are moaning about the rain, the cold, the course, the changing facilities or any other combination. You have to sign on so you have to be social in some way but negativity can only be a bad thing.

A fundamental truth is that negativity attracts negativity in all walks of life and that is the last thing you need before your event especially if you were just thinking yourself how yuck it is out there. What you need is self-motivation and a self-defence policy to beat off the negative vibes round about you. You have to remember that there are competitors out there who will deliberately try to demotivate other riders by sounding negative about everything. The majority, though, will whinge simply because they just don't realise the damage they are doing to their own chances and, ironically, seek out others of similar minds for comfort.

> ## if you need to respond to negative comments, my favoured line in the past was 'ah well, it'll be what it is'

A lot of races are won or lost before the start line, and here are a few ideas I put into practice over the years. The first point of defence is against your own instinctive and socially trained reaction to bad news, which is to react by projecting how bad it is going to be for you. That might be the weather forecast the evening before or course route details. Don't think of yourself – think of the other riders and how much they won't like it. You can do this with everything and allocate the bad stuff to others and the good stuff like downhill and tailwind to yourself. You must will it to be the worst and think to yourself 'bring it on', knowing how badly it will affect your rivals.

The best way to deal with negative types is twofold. Firstly, think to yourself how much they have talked themselves out of a good ride, and secondly, politely excuse yourself, and if you need to respond to negative comments, my favoured line in the past was 'ah well, it'll be what it is'. You can produce an off-the-cuff line of your own but it has to be able to be said while walking away from them and it cannot accept or agree with the negative comments. Whatever you do, *do not* try and work out their motives – it is too distracting and anyhow the whole negative psychology won't work on you while you are taking comfort from it.

A good policy is to get to know the riders that are always upbeat. Hang about after rides and get chatting to some of the older riders that might be at other events. Usually they are pretty hardy and will return an upbeat comment with the same. It is a good thing if you can have some verbal interaction with positive people before your ride since the same is true that positivity attracts positivity. Even in a social setting if someone opens with a negative then the response is usually mirrored, and the same is true of positivity. That is why it's so good to find a reliable upbeat group and be positive. All you will get back is more positivity. There is a part of the human psyche that accepts suffering in company easier than alone. If you let your subconscious know that someone else is struggling on with a smile in the face of adversity, then that is a powerful source of mental strength.

A very important thing to develop is your own routine both the evening before and on the day of the event itself. A good idea is to write an itinerary of everything you need for your event then pack everything the evening before. It is not good to be lying in bed thinking I must remember this or that thing in the morning. A routine in the morning of the event is good because it almost becomes ritualistic and becomes part of the focusing process.

This can involve warming up on your turbo, what and when you want to eat, etc. It seems a strange thing to suggest but occasionally doing a fake pre-race routine before going on a training ride with the actual food and fluids you would consume, an actual (fake) start time and toilet break is a good idea. When you go to an event and you know exactly your preparatory build-up, it is a bit like a comfort blanket because it has become routine. The more things that are familiar to you at an event, the more relaxed and focused you will be in an alien environment.

PRE-RACE POSITIVE THINKING

- Avoid negative people where possible and try to get to know the upbeat 'old stager' types
- With any adversity in your event – think about the other riders
- Develop your own pre-event routine

A problem a lot of riders can have is not being able to sleep well the night before. This can cause a spiral of worry where lack of sleep makes you fear that your chance of a good result is slipping away, which in turn causes more worry and nervousness. The point that you need to take on board to tackle the syndrome is that lack of sleep has almost no effect on sporting performance in a one-day event provided you have lain still through the night. So no point in worrying about a loss of physical ability whether you sleep well or not. Another interesting factor to note in the battle against nerves is that the experience is very close to the emotion of excitement, close enough that we can convince ourselves that in fact this is what we are feeling – ahead of our good result to come.

A major source of nervousness is not the fear of the result itself but the thought that you will not be able to give it your best in the event. A conscious decision that you will accept the result whatever it is always helps. A look at the wider perspective of family and friends that a bad result would mean in that context helps at that very moment. In other words, no one will die and you won't lose your house.

These thought processes are good at reassuring us, but by far the best system is to make the event seem further away in your mind. I already

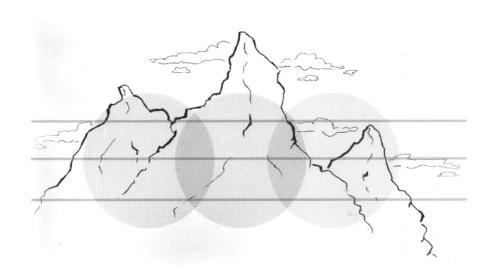

mentioned the pre-race routine, and one other reason I think it is important is that if you visualise everything you have to do before you even get to the start including that routine, then that start seems further away in event time. The subconscious mind does not run on chronological time but by event-to-event time – and putting on a sock or switching on a kettle or reaching for a cup are all 'events'. I used to imagine all the tiniest things like putting each sock on, going to the toilet, switching on the kettle, etc, etc. Bear in mind that nervousness is an emotion that is related to fear of an impending event and the level of nervousness is related to how imminent that event is (how many events come before it). Your thinking higher consciousness cannot control it directly. However, if your thinking self can make the event seem a whole lot less imminent than it is by thinking of all those many, many events that take place first, it can only help reduce the problem. I used to sleep soundly after perfecting this technique. I am not aware of scientific studies so I can only recommend what worked for me.

TO AVOID SLEEPLESSNESS
* Realise that loss of sleep won't wreck your performance
* Try relating nervousness to the feeling of excitement
* Think of all the things you have to do before you even start

The idea of preparing psychologically to do what is fundamentally a physical activity may seem strange to some people, but when you consider that the dividing line between the good and the great is their mental strength and determination, then it makes sense. When you consider that the mind is an organ like any other that needs training to perform at its best and when you consider the importance of the cognitive and subconscious mind in achieving great physical feats then it is not a statement too far to say that the making of a champion is the mind of a champion. *Make your mind work for you!*

IN BRIEF

Good thoughts in preparation for an event will consolidate all your other training activity. Never underestimate the importance of working to understand, strengthen and train the thought process – this is a fundamental part of training which is often overlooked.

- A thought is like a thing, real, tangible with the power to influence change
- Be committed to a more productive and accurate attitude
- We have control over our performance by the way we think
- Believe in your potential and cultivate the confidence that you can do better

Psychology of racing

When it comes to the day of the big event there is nothing more you can do to improve your physical ability. Your level of fitness and physical potential is what it is. Your equipment and build-up to the event is in place. Your cake is baked already and all that you can do now is take away from your best possible result. The only thing you can change now is how you think. How you think and how well prepared you are mentally will affect how you act and react to the environment and people around you between arriving at the event and crossing the finish line. The focus of your mind is actually the only variable. Barring bad luck, how you think and act will determine whether you reach your personal potential or fall short.

The Corinthian spirit, or the ideology that just taking part is the foremost important factor, is common among amateur sports people. This is a resolve-sapping malaise that primes the mind for underperformance, not just the thinking self but the subconscious mind that does not normally hold sporting success high up in the hierarchy of need. By that I mean food, shelter, social standing, sex, etc. The idea that it is OK to not reach your full potential is not a good thought to have when you are doing the ride and reaching within yourself for extra effort.

> barring bad luck, how you think and act will determine whether you reach your personal potential or fall short

This ideology is not just an influence from others that passes viral-like from person to person. This spirit is part of us as in most non-sporting activities whether it be decorating, cleaning or whatever, even work-related things, we reach a point where we think the outcome is good enough and move on. What we don't tend to do is openly question in our thinking minds whether it is the best we can do. When it is good enough we just move on to something else. This is normal and indeed healthy for general life in society. The alternative would be obsessive-compulsive disorder or something similar. This is our behavioural pattern, our lifestyle habit.

The Corinthian spirit is only a verbal reminder of what is our natural way. At some point and to a varying degree, the idea that just having a go is fine must have been part of a thought process that allowed you to take up a sport in the first instance. Few of us would take up a sport with the inner belief that we must do our absolute best always. We give ourselves some slack, just as we would expect and encourage a newcomer to a sport with the 'just have a go' philosophy.

This raises a question we have to ask ourselves: if we have never actually addressed the issue and consciously dismissed this attitude or replaced it with a new one, then what remains of it? More than anything else, does it reside in the back of our minds ready to trip us up when the going gets too tough, too unbearable?

Clearly then the competitive event is an environment where we have to set aside our natural way in order to make the most of our potential. We need to be able to set aside the philosophy that serves us well in general life for the time that we are being competitive. We can train our ability to block out negative thought processes by the way we allow ourselves to think when we are in the sporting environment and when we are in the company of others. There is the matter of blocking out any negative or capitulatory ideology but also the need to build up an attitude that compels us to proactively make our best performance happen.

The first important thing to be dealt with is establishing prime motives. What is it that drives us to be competitive, to take part in events that test our ability and measure it against others? This level of self-analysis is rarely undertaken by the majority of riders, mainly because it is a mental exercise that we rarely undertake in normal life. There is also the deterrent that deep self-analysis is a difficult and sometimes painful task that requires honesty. This can take us out of a comfort zone where we drift along by force of habit and simple repetition of what we always did. We hope to reach into ourselves and ask: why do I ride to try to be better than other people, what is the emotional gain from doing so?

You could disappear into a corner right now and have a Zen moment of total self-understanding, but it is unlikely. Let me help you along the path by asking if you are actually competitive at all? A lot of people take part in competitive events and 'compete' because it makes them part of a peer group doing the same. That is not to say that they don't turn up and

ride at their best perceived effort. It just means that one of their major motivations for taking part will be satisfied with a good or average result. This is not wrong since we are gregarious animals and this is high up in our hierarchy of need for general life. This also does not mean that you cannot be genuinely competitive by digging even deeper into motive and allowing yourself to be more in touch with more proactive driving forces. It also helps to make clear in your mind the points in time before and after the actual doing part of the competition as being a distinct, separate and completely different part of the competitive experience. Being part of the racing community and the social aspect of the competition is a good motive to hold on to, as long as it can be replaced by completely competitive motives at the point of action. The race itself is a time totally separate from the rest of life and needs a different set of motives and values if we are to bring out our best performances.

So being part of a community and peer group is a good umbrella motive but it must be put on hold and replaced by new motives at the point of action. It will take further self-analysis to dig into why we want to produce better results. There are two sides to the outcome of a race and what satisfies us in regard to our performance. There is the personal satisfaction of our performance in terms of self-respect, self-worth, perceived social status, vanity, ego, bragging rights, etc., and there is the thought process of others such as respect, admiration, etc. Both of these are actually part of the same motive that is self-satisfaction since the altered perception of others is part of the satisfaction that we feel. We have to ask ourselves whether we are driven by the desire to beat other people (or one person in particular) or by the desire to be the best that we can be for ourselves as measured against our best potential result. The desire to beat an opponent has been a good motivator for a lot of people, but fundamentally it is a negative motive since it is based upon the principle outcome being someone else's demise. If you truly detest someone and provided they turn up at your event, then the drive for vengeance can be very powerful, but in most cases it is a negative distraction from your own performance. The more you think about other riders the less you are thinking about what you are doing to produce your own best performance. It is important to have it clear in your mind that your performance is by you, for you. The others have no bearing on what you physically do – only you do by focusing solely on *you*. The others may affect your race by their actions and how you must react but that reaction is decided and executed only by you, for the best result that you can do. Make you and your best effort the centre of your motive and you have a new and more powerful opponent to battle at every event – yourself. A battle between what your potential is and what you actually do. This self-driven motivation is even more important when it comes to making improvements in training efforts. We can merge both sides by thinking that by using a motive based on our own best effort for ourselves we will reach our best performance that will inevitably beat our rivals anyhow. First and foremost we must think of our effort for our benefit.

When it comes to the build-up to the race itself, it's good to think of being part of the event and that there will be a bit of a social element after the recovering is done, but we must be clear in our minds that when it comes to the doing part of it our psychology and way of thinking has to flip to a different attitude. I spoke earlier about avoiding negative influences round about us before the start of an event, and it is important as part of our preparation to do what we can to feel as confident as possible. No one at an event can undermine our confidence about our ability on the day provided we don't let them!

An important part of this is making sure your own equipment is as good as it can be mechanically and set up exactly the way you want it for the performance you expect to output. It is important to have your race machine as clean as possible and your race kit washed clean. Even the clothes you arrive in should be as smart as possible within the context of a sports event. People who wear smart clothes feel more confident and less intimidated by people round about them. Having your equipment spotlessly clean and the tyres checked for faults, the chain cleaned and re-oiled will make you feel better prepared. Remind yourself that the position on your bike is now exactly where you need it. I say this since it is easy to look at more expensive kit and feel you are at a disadvantage.

A truth about racing bikes is that the difference between good kit and exceptional kit is actually very little despite what the industry wants us to believe. The largest difference by far is correct positioning and crank length and reminding yourself of that fact before the event will deflect the undermining effect of seeing someone else with super-expensive equipment. A good policy is to avoid looking closely at other people's bikes before an event and concentrate on your perfect-fitting machine and the ride you intend to do on it. On the day of the event it is good policy to move straight onto your preparation and warm-up routine.

Another thing that can have a negative influence is the thought of a previous ride that was less than your best. There is a saying in sport that you are only as good as your last ride. If that is true then it is also true that you are only as good as your *next* ride, and this is your next ride. Stay in the present, and while you are warming up remember that the past is gone and if you have seen improvement in your turbo power output then you can be confident that that is real and take assurance from it. The other thing is to remind yourself how much time and effort you have put in just to be this ready on this start line.

I say this because I have observed a phenomenon where the degree of effort and determination a rider puts in is proportional to how far they have had to travel to be at the event. Not just distance but time and expense. This is most noticeable with riders from island communities, who quite often have to travel the day before an event and stay over. Such riders usually display dogged determination not to give up or slack off no matter the circumstances. They usually perform better in comparison to the average rider that lives nearby with similar ability because they have invested so much time and effort just to be there. The difference can be explained in terms of how much we value something that is readily available and cheap against something that is rare and expensive. In other words if we can travel easily to loads of races then we value each opportunity to ride less than someone who rarely has the chance. The expression 'easy come, easy go' springs to mind in describing this syndrome.

This value system is not a good philosophy when it comes to pulling every bit of our potential effort out on the day if we are one of those fortunate enough to have easy access to loads of events. The very knowledge that our access to a lot of races can undermine our level of commitment is the first step towards countering it. The importance of this is not just the desire to perform at our level best in the present event. It is important to develop a racing frame of mind where giving up or not reaching totally into ourselves becomes a thought or reaction process that no longer exists in our options menu when we are faced with adversity. The more often we race with an island philosophy, the more alien the bail-out option becomes.

> **if you visualise riding hard and breathing correctly, pedalling perfectly and getting a good result, then this lays down the foundation for your mind to make your imagined effort and result come true**

In the build-up to the event and especially on the day itself, it is a good thing to think over all the sacrifices and training rides that you had to do to be here at this one race as well as the expense. This is a means of generating an island philosophy that we deservedly should have when we add up exactly what it costs us to be here, right now. Think of all that as you warm up and visualise a possible point in the event where you might otherwise cave in, like losing contact with a group and imagine

+ create your perfect fitting machine +

being that island rider giving totally everything you have to overcome it. Remember, everyone can always do more than they think they can, and using psychological techniques like priming your mind and concentrating on how so very much this actual race matters, you can push yourself closer to your actual limit. In an actual race situation you can visualise an island rider beside you in the same state as yourself and vow to give up when he would. It is a good thing to imagine yourself in that situation beforehand and how you would ride longer and harder than you otherwise would. It is a strange thing to visualise yourself visualising, but this generates a prearranged fallback position in your mind that you would not go to normally in the exhaustion of battle.

It is also important to think only about this one race and not about other events in the past or to come. If you are thinking about the event you are at as being good preparation for an event to come, then it suddenly becomes less of a preparation since you will scale back the desire and perhaps event goals. The best way to prepare for an upcoming event that you know is more important than the one you are presently at is not to think of any other race. Think: this is the one and only race. If your mind wanders off thinking about other races, instantly pull it back to the present and how you have invested so much into this one event. Think: this is right here right now, I must reach my potential.

Visualisation is a very powerful method of training your mind to behave in certain ways in certain situations. If you visualise riding so hard and breathing correctly, pedalling perfectly and getting a good result, then this lays down the foundation for your mind to make your imagined effort and result come true. If you visualise a level of effort and discomfort as well as the result in a dreamlike visual imagining often enough, then this can become a self-fulfilling prophecy in a positive way. If you allow your mind to wander into imagining a bad result, then this too could lead to your inner mind guiding you to that very result in the real world.

Visualisation might seem to be just playing mind games but it can actually have a real physiological impact. I explained earlier about how the brain and nervous system use electrical pulses to control our bodies. While we imagine our muscles pedalling and our lungs breathing, the control pathways in our brain that make those things happen are stimulated and made stronger. The impulse signals become more dependable and stronger and the pathways to the rest of our body become more efficient. As well as that, tactical situations and how we react to them can become second nature. Situations where we imagine we are totally spent but carry on regardless can be ingrained in us at a subconscious level. Because we become more exhausted in a race and the lack of oxygen to the brain can impair our clear decision-making ability, it is important that our predetermined decision not to give in or slack off is ingrained at a deeper level.

Visualisation is something that expands beyond race-day preparation and into the world of preparing for training, etc. It is useful to imagine going to the venue for the race and meeting people who may be a positive or negative influence that day. If you visualise yourself using your warm-up and being positive and thinking about the thing already outlined – about how you are racing against your own potential and that your position is perfect and your speed index on your turbo said you're good and you do this for you and your own feeling of success – then this whole attitude will be primed to be upon you when you do your usual warm-up routine. It is the most basic psychology, but Pavlov showed that by ringing a bell while feeding dogs he could make them salivate by only ringing the bell. You will be able by habit of routine to be in a state of mind so that you will ride this day as though it is the major ride to come. A positive and trained mindset cannot guarantee victory but a negative one will almost certainly result in failure.

IN BRIEF

How you think can and will determine whether you ever get near your true and absolute potential. Real athletic confidence is built upon a complicated foundation of training, diet and rest. The actions of the mind determine the winners from the rest.

- **Stay in the present – your performance is about today, not last week or last year**
- **Meticulous attention to equipment choice and detail is vital to ensure your confidence is based upon event planning to complement your training programme**
- **We all have an options menu; learn to challenge the option that says 'I have tried hard enough' – there is always, regardless how small, some gas left in the tank**
- **Visualisation is of great value, learning how to put your mind in the situation of a race day scenario**

Breathing

I can say with conviction that breathing is an activity that we have all been doing since we were born. Otherwise known as respiration, it is a process of inhaling and exhaling air in order to oxygenate the blood through the membrane of the lungs. That we have been doing this for so long, and the fact that it is usually a bodily function not controlled by a minute-to-minute thought process, suggests that few of us will have stopped to question the way we breathe. This is such a life or death activity that it cannot be left to our thinking selves to remember to keep doing it.

It is so essential to life that we are hard-wired to breath in and out from our first moments of life outside the womb. Evolution has led us to breathe rhythmically and continuously throughout our lives with hardly a thought given to it, unless we are faced with a moment of suffocation, asthma, drowning, childbirth or the like. This has been essential because a baby has to breathe from the start and there is no opportunity or need to teach breathing technique. Evolution favours the simple solution, which is clearly breathing in and out with a feedback mechanism that prevents over-oxygenation and under-oxygenation of the blood.

> the fact remains that breathing in
> and out rhythmically in a better way
> is still the equivalent of honing the
> doggy paddle

I compare this evolutionary in-built response (the need to breath) to that of swimming. If a child or even a cat or dog falls into deep water, they will survive by doing the doggy-paddle. This is not trained – it is hard wired. I make this comparison in order to show that an evolutionary response is not necessarily the most efficient solution to our needs in response to environmental conditions. Clearly, having used our intelligence and ability to analyse and invent, we have devised strokes and trained ourselves to swim far better than the manner instinct alone has provided us with. The same too is true of breathing. In terms of bicycle riding, the environmental condition dictates the need for the maximum intake of oxygen and the instinctive response is breathing harder and more rapidly – gasping. I assert that neither breathing harder nor doggy-paddling harder will match an intelligent trained response to those environmental needs. Bearing in mind that oxygen intake is usually the limiting factor in how hard we can ride, especially during aerobic threshold sessions on the turbo, then persevering with the breathing technique to follow is paramount to gaining between 3 per cent and 8 per cent instant advantage depending on how good your technique is, according to tests carried out by myself and close friends.

until this publication only three other individuals knew the secret Obree method

The first thing to say about this is that, no matter how well honed and controlled your breathing technique is, it involves breathing in and out rhythmically. All mammals do this, but a lot of athletes and cyclists have trained themselves to breath in a way that maximises the efficiency of the lungs, by not gasping and using the nasal passages to help maximise the efficient intake of air for example. These techniques are useful in stepping forward from how instinct alone would have us respond and so are valuable and worth taking on. I will guide you through them, but the fact remains that breathing in and out rhythmically in a better way is still the equivalent of honing the doggy-paddle. The ultimate solution I have formulated after a lot of research and anecdotal testing and experimentation is the three-phase Obree breathing pattern. The full cycle of normal breathing is also referred to as three-phase, as in exhalation, pause, inhalation. This Obree method involves three whole breaths. This is my equivalent to the front crawl. Having some of my peer group test this yet keep it secret from my rivals and foreign federations was difficult, and until this publication only three other individuals knew of this. I will guide you through step by step.

Firstly, you must learn the best technique in the field of instinctive breathing since these also help maximise the 3-phase pattern. Assuming no previous thought on breath control then it is likely you would take more

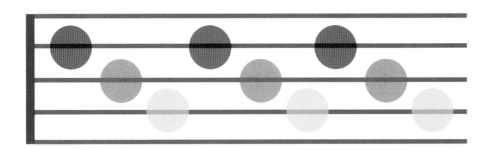

frequent breaths through the mouth as the demand for oxygen rises. The best way to breathe is to have more controlled, slightly deeper breaths where we breathe out only through our mouths and back in through the mouth and nasal passages. Do not spend effort working out how deeply to breath since we will move on from that to the three-phase pattern. Concentrate on breathing out through mouth and in through mouth and nose.

If you want to take this to the gold standard, then there are two other things needing doing at the same time. Flaring your nostrils outwards during intake will aid air flow and the reason it is important to use the nasal passages to their maximum is because these are lined with blood vessels to heat the air on the way through. This not only helps heat the air but also helps the body lose excess heat. The heating of the air causes the oxygen molecules to move about faster, increasing uptake in the lungs. The other thing you must do during intake is put the tip of your tongue on the roof of your mouth so that the air passes over the underside of your tongue, also helping to heat and moisturise the air. The tongue must then be returned to its flat position during exhalation.

If it has not been complicated enough, there is the question of how we set about the job of inhaling and exhaling all together. If no thought is given to it, then we will instinctively use intercostals and diaphragm muscles as well as some in the neck and shoulders. To develop a better breathing technique, while maintaining all the actions above, try using the abdominal muscles to pull and push the bottom of the lungs in conjunction with raising and lowering the chest cavity. The good news is that you can practise and perfect this away from the sporting arena. You can do this while watching the TV or during a quiet time at work. Here is a quick recap of the technique. It might be worthwhile engaging with this technique until it has become a force of habit when called on to be used – a bit like learning an instrument, learning this part properly before moving on to the next lesson.

- Breathing in – flare nostrils and put tip of tongue on roof of mouth, use mouth and nose, use abdominal muscles
- Breathing out – put tongue flat and exhale only via mouth, use some abdominal muscles to pump the lungs like bellows

Because the act of breathing is so instinctive and because the previous habit of a lifetime has been to take rhythmic breaths of much the same size, this could be a very challenging change to adopt for many people. I spent a lot of time experimenting to find the best strategy but once I settled on this method I used it when riding at all times until it became automatic, and the actual period of time before I did not have to actively think hard about each next breath was relatively short, a month or so. Now I use this three-breath pattern all the time.

BAD AIR

- to -

GOOD AIR

Just as I explained about breathing being instinctive and not necessarily the best way, I think it is important to explain the science as I go into the details of the three-breath technique because the more you believe in it, the more you will invest in it. For a start, it may intuitively seem less efficient in terms of oxygen uptake not taking each breath as hard as possible, but let me expand upon the inefficiencies in instinctual exhalation and inhalation and how these can be compensated. At the start of this chapter I wrote about 'inhaling *and* exhaling' explicitly because we think first of inhaling as our primal motive in getting oxygen into our lungs. A drowning person rarely thinks of exhaling as a priority, and it is a common mistake in this situation to keep trying to breathe more air into already full lungs. My point is that we have to start by changing our mindset and think of breathing as a process of exhaling followed by inhaling. Getting rid of oxygen-depleted air is the most important part of the respiration cycle.

Lungs are like bellows that waft air out and in through a single hole – the throat. All the while oxygen is being taken out of whatever air exists in the lungs and carbon dioxide is taken up by the lungs from the body in a process called 'gas exchange'. In studying this it became clear that as the quantity of oxygen left in the air decreases so does the rate of uptake. To compound the problem, the less inflated the lungs the less uptake can take place. Bearing in mind the lung is a bag that deflates and inflates through a single hole then the solution is to breathe out the bad air and take in a new load, as nature has us do.

There is a major problem, and compromise, in the process of rhythmic breathing in that complete deflation would leave a long period of very low gas exchange yet partial deflation leaves a lot of oxygen-diminished air still in the lungs that simply mixes with the fresh air to form a body of partially depleted air. In normal breathing for an exercising athlete what we get is about a one-third deflation of the lungs – expelling one-third of the lungs' air per exhalation – in a cycle that has two-thirds of the original air remain with each breath. This is nature's compromise within the constraint of rhythmic breathing.

Clearly if we allow ourselves as thinking mammals to move away from rhythmic breathing then we can formulate a breathing pattern that optimises the best part of the respiration cycle. The best way to optimise oxygen exchange is to maximise the amount of time that the lung has good air at near full inflation against the time that it is nearly deflated with bad air. Here is how it works.

For the first breath of the three-breath pattern you start from reasonably full lungs then exhale strongly and much further than you would normally exhale then inhale to a slightly greater depth than normal. At this point you have as much oxygenated air as possible in as inflated as possible lungs. Clearly repeating this in a rhythmic pattern would be unsustainable and inefficient, thus nature's compromise as I just mentioned. I have to make clear that this is not a breath out and in to the absolute limit of the lungs but rather a good breath out and a good breath in.

The second breath is a half breath or less. It requires you to partially exhale and then inhale almost to where you were or just a little short of it. You should still have more inflated lungs than during your instinctive breathing pattern. This allows some exchange of air while keeping the lungs mainly inflated.

The third breath should be a little breath. It requires you to exhale perhaps a quarter breath or so and then inhale a little before beginning the sequence again. At this point the air will have been deoxygenated to the point where a maximum refill of fresh air is required. This is the most important part of the entire phase and how well you concentrate on exhaling the bad air dictates the amount of oxygen in the fully inflated lungs. This is why I made the point earlier that you must have the expulsion of bad air as your priority.

THE THREE-BREATH BREATHING PATTERN

- Full breath out (the most important part), full breath in
- Half breath out, similar breath back in
- Quarter breath out, breath back in a little

Bear it in mind that you also must maintain the nostril and tongue technique at the same time. If previous to reading this chapter you had only used the gasping system, then doing all this simultaneously may seem daunting, but when you consider the effort of learning the front crawl from the doggy-paddle then the same input would give you this system. If that was your starting point, then the advantage would be as significant.

Another point to make about this Obree technique is that it masks the feeling of being out of breath to some degree because most of the bad air is replaced by good air in one go so the body's own feedback system is duped a little into thinking the carbon dioxide level in the body is less than it is. This means not only that we can have more oxygen delivered to our bloodstream but that we can push ourselves further before our body tells us we cannot work any harder.

In extreme efforts it is important to keep concentrating on the breathing rhythm, the speed, pace and feel of the breathing cycle. You may be tempted to resort to gasping for breath in extreme situations, for instance, a hill climb, but this will be counterproductive. I go back to the effort to exert your thinking upon the athletic demands and ensure all of the training cycle comes to bear in the most extreme situations. Clearly there will come a point where athletic improvement is impossible due to the inability of your athletic system to supply or convert sufficient oxygen. We seldom push our bodies to this level, but if your effort is that intense, bear in mind the breathing technique will make more oxygen available to your aerobic system and therefore enable improved athletic response to that situation.

This technique may allow people to exercise harder than ever before, and it is important that this be taken into consideration in terms of health before embarking upon it. There is much to gain from this so please do persevere – at your own risk!

IN BRIEF

Normal breathing patterns operate adequately when our bodies are in a non-stressed condition but during athletic pursuit breathing can be improved dramatically by our taking conscious control of the breathing cycle. The Obree breathing pattern is a three-phase controlled respiratory cycle which optimises the delivery of oxygen supply therefore creating the conditions for improved athletic output.

- Think about the process of breathing in via the mouth and nose
- Use the abdominal muscles to pump the lungs like bellows to drive out old used air
- Learn to follow the Obree breathing pattern and it will soon become normal to you

Pedalling

The act of pedalling produces two forms of energy, heat and movement. Heat is created naturally as a result of muscle movement and the fact that the conversion of food stores in the body to kinetic energy (movement) is not 100 per cent efficient. The amount of heat produced in relation to the energy transmitted through the rotation of the cranks is the measure of efficiency. You would be forgiven for thinking that pedalling is such a simple act that the efficiency of it is what it is and there is not much we can do about it. That is not the case and quite often the divide that separates equally talented opponents is not who can produce the most amount of energy, but who can waste the least. The entire quest in looking at the pedalling action and retraining our technique is to have the largest proportion of our precious energy as possible go into producing movement.

Everybody who rides a bike knows how to pedal just the same as anybody who does not drown in deep water knows how to swim. The fundamental problem with pedalling is that the pedals bowl round and round whether you pedal in a good way or not and bad technique looks no different from good technique. I make the analogy to swimming again in this chapter because the complexity of pedalling with optimum efficiency is probably as complex and engaging as learning a good stroke from a bad one. In swimming, a poor technique would be instantly noticeable and correctable to the trained eye, and more to the point, the swimmer would be eager to improve technically since success would be impossible otherwise.

The majority of cyclists on the other hand learn to ride a bike as children and don't think about the detail of the pedal action at any point. Where it is an absolute priority in swimming to improve technically at all levels of the sport, this has not been the case in the world of cycling. Even at elite level it has been quite rare to investigate the entire pedal action to the degree that a swimmer will eagerly pursue every possibility of improvement. This problem, apart from firstly having to convince the rider that it is essential, is that the entrenched habitual pedalling signals from the brain have to be untrained while a new set of impulses are learned. Just like the breathing technique, this is similar to trying to teach someone to play a musical instrument correctly who has been playing it wrongly all their life. That person is you, and if you open your mind to learn a more complex sequence of muscle stimuli that will produce more movement, less heat and less muscle strain, then you open yourself up to the possibility of a considerable improvement in performance.

The first thing you need to know is the basic physics involved in the transfer of energy. Almost everything in cycling can be explained by physiology and physics and it is important to get a handle on the basic principles. The governing factor on how fast you can go is not strength or how much force can be brought down on the pedals – it is the energy. When I tell you later on to pedal with less force it is not necessary that you understand the physics but that you believe it. Nonetheless here is the physics of it.

The pedal is the object being moved in a circular direction. The amount of energy transferred to it is simply the amount of force applied to it multiplied by the distance travelled. It is slightly more complicated than that because it is the force pushing the pedal forward that counts. What this means is that a smaller force applied to the pedal in a forward motion for a greater distance travelled can produce more energy than a large force for a shorter distance. In other words a rider with weaker muscles in terms of absolute strength can produce more power and more speed than a stronger rider if he uses more of the pedalling circle more effectively. By 'effectively' I mean by applying a force as near to the forward motion as possible.

shoes that inhibit ankle flexibility in any way will also inhibit your pedal stroke

The first step in putting this into action is having the right equipment and pedal adjustment. Shoes are probably the most important part of your equipment and the only piece of equipment professional riders carry with them as hand luggage and for good reason. The placement of the plate is vitally important and should be set so that the centre of the pedal is below the ball of the foot. It is also a good policy to get a pedal system that offers the least amount of stack height – this is the distance between the centre of the pedal and the sole of the shoe. It is not that important that you should go and spend a load of money to replace your existing pedal set-up but if you

find yourself looking for better pedals, this has to be the number one priority. I must mention that if you end up with lower stack height, you must lower your seat accordingly and perhaps your handlebars too.

As far as shoes go it is worth paying a little extra to get a pair with carbon-fibre soles. Not only are they lighter and less flexible but the sole is thinner which also effectively reduces the stack height. The importance of shoes cannot be overstated since all your energy must be transferred through them to the pedals. How shoes fit is a very personal thing and I would advise trying lots of pairs at different outlets to be sure of perfect fit since different manufacturers work to different templates. The main difference to be on the lookout for is the width. Italian manufacturers tend to make narrower shoes whereas others may be average or wider. You may be wary of shoes that have tightening devices very high up on the arches. I will stress the importance of ankle flexibility later on, and a pair of shoes that inhibit that in any way will also inhibit your pedal stroke. I have removed pieces from the top of almost every pair of shoes I have ever owned, and the usual problem has been the length of the tongue. Greg Lemond, three times Tour de France winner, used to add and remove bits of his shoes and would always use that one pair when he knew he had got them right. You don't have to go to these lengths but be sure to shop around.

The next link in the order of importance is the crank arms and it is important that they are not too long. There has been a trend towards longer cranks in the belief this will give more leverage and therefore more power. This is not true because beyond a certain length there is a drop-off in the amount of the pedalling circle that can be used effectively. Remember the force × distance rule of energy – less use of stroke equals less energy. I am 1m 80cm and use 170mm cranks. I went to 172.5mm cranks and found they were too long. You can do a pro-rata calculation, but if you are shorter than this but have longer cranks, it is likely that you need to go shorter to take advantage of the technique I am about to explain. If you do triathlon, then this is even more important since overlong cranks promote a slower pedalling rate and more pushing force from the muscles, which is not a good thing before the run.

Lastly, the saddle position has to be looked at to find the best place in both height and how far back it is. This will be a whole new way of pedalling so it may require a whole new saddle position! There has been a trend in general towards having saddles further and further forward. This is not a good trend, especially if you do sportives and longer road events. Aside from the efficiency factor there is general comfort and balance of the body's mass to gain from trying to get your saddle further back. A forward saddle causes a lot of weight to fall on the arms and shoulders. If you suffer from a stiff neck during or after riding, then there is a good chance that this is a major contributor. Experiment with your saddle position and do not be afraid to take it back by quite a chunk – my own bike has a saddle tip more than 10cm behind the bracket. If you do, then you also have to lower height. A good rule of thumb is to lower one part for every four parts moved back. As you go through the process of learning the riding style to follow, you may naturally find yourself sitting further back on the saddle and, if so, move it accordingly.

PEDALLING SET-UP

- Check out your crank length compared to your height (as a guide: 9.5 per cent of height)
- Make sure your pedal spindle is directly below the ball of your foot
- Be prepared to move your saddle about
- Make sure your shoes do not impede free ankle movement

The basic principles of using the full pedal cycle are relatively simple. The difficult part is learning to use it on the bike all the time without having to think deeply about every single pedal stroke. At the start you will have to do just that to replace your old pedalling habit with a better one. When I set out on this quest in the late 1980s, it took at least a month before it became my new way. This will take perseverance and on top of the breathing technique you can understand better why I said near the start of this book that there is enough to think about on the bike without the need for computers and heart monitors. I can also tell you that if you follow my stretching routine on a daily basis, this technique will just seem to get easier and easier. If you master this, then you will never go back to the old way.

The first point of the stroke is when the cranks are straight up and down (top dead centre). This is the most neglected part of the stroke and conventional thinking is that you have to wait until your legs have bowled past to 30° or 40° before applying a proper standing force on the pedal. This is where we must learn to use the most neglected muscle in cycling, the vastus medial – the muscle you kick a football with. You have to start at the top by kicking that football. On the upstroke leading up to this point you should have allowed your ankle to drop so that your foot is at an acute angle to your shin (hence the need for free movement).

This is not an explosive kick, but because your ankle is dropped, you roll onto where you would normally put the force down and use the available movement in the ankle to employ the calf muscles as well as the muscles in the thigh to drive the pedal stroke downwards. This enables you to use the entire half circle of the downward stroke. At the start you will need to do this in slow motion to get to grips with it, but if you think L—O—N—G (as in the stroke) it will keep you focused on distance of stroke rather than force during the long downstroke. Don't try to put one burst of strength at the middle point. This is about using just a little less force than a stomping style but delivering it evenly over a long stroke. Because the peak force is less than before there is the advantage that fatigue is also less, even though more power is being outputted.

There are two distinct halves to this stroke, and the second is the upstroke where you pull the ankle back to a dipped position ready for the next kick forward. Perfect timing can make such a difference to the fluidity and power of this stroke action. Ideally, the second leg is kicking its football just as the first leg has finished its long stroke and is moving for the upstroke. A slight lateral rocking style helps this technique to work, and if you achieve good timing then you will find this incredibly useful on a long climb. I should point out here that a lot of riders have developed a bad habit of dropping their shoulders with every pedal stroke, which leads to an ungainly upper body movement. Most people will have seen cyclists who have developed this habit and ride with an erratic, overcompensating upper torso and shoulder movement. When I was much younger I did this as well but overcame it by putting that action into my pedals at the exact moment that my shoulder would have dropped and found an instant benefit. It is one of those cases of engrained habit that can be hard to break – but it can be done. It has to be since this long stroke just will not work with shoulder-drop syndrome. I'll mention it in another chapter, but keeping your head always in the same line holds everything in rhythm while you use a rocking style. As you get better at this, you may find that you want to put the saddle even further back to get behind the pedals and that you can kick forward before the crank is even vertical.

You might want to practise this on the turbo in slow motion.

PEDAL STROKE TECHNIQUE

- Start with you heel dropped with the cranks vertical
- Kick that football and follow through with calf and thigh muscles
- Think L—O—N—G stroke
- Kick with your opposite leg just as you go to pull for the upstroke
- Slightly rock onto each pedal

Out of the saddle effort is a different matter since it is more difficult to control the kick stroke (when the crank is vertical). It is possible to use it to some degree but nowhere near to the effect of the in-saddle effort, and when you

Kick forward

Engage calf muscle and think long stroke

Switch to pulling toe up at same moment as kicking

Pulling toe up as much as possible

eventually (yes – eventually you can do this) perfect the in-saddle technique you will find yourself using the out-of-saddle effort less often simply because on a long climb it is less efficient and on the flat it is less aerodynamic.

There are times when an out-of-saddle effort is required, for a change of pace or on a very steep part of a climb, for example. The most common fault on such an effort is applying the downward force too late in the stroke. It is essential to step on the pedal as soon as it reaches the sweet spot, which is when the crank gets to about 45° past vertical. If you can manage the kick on the out-of-saddle effort then follow through, that's great, but it is not an easy skill to master.

Catching the crank at the sweet spot is the most important thing but control of the upper body is also essential. A lot of energy can be lost by using the arms to pull and heave on the bar. That serves no purpose other than to twist the front end of the bike. Anticipating what size of gear you will need in advance will help reduce this, but there are always times when we get caught out. On such occasions it is a good idea to have your arms as straight as possible to reduce muscle strain and allow yourself as straight a spine as your bike position will allow, but not locked totally straight as that is dangerous.

OUT-OF-SADDLE EFFORT

- Try to engage the pedal early on the downstroke
- Keep arms as straight as possible – but not locked straight
- Train yourself not to bounce erratically
- Use the calf muscles
- Ride in the saddle whenever you can

It is also important not to bounce up and down since this also wastes energy and spoils the smooth flow of your pedal action. You can practise this by putting noisy things like coins in your back pockets and ride out-of-the-saddle in a way that they don't rattle. Concentrate on dual timing with one leg kicking down just as the other is pulling up while being conscious about engaging the calf muscles in the process. There is always a temptation to allow the shoulders to bounce up and down and to pull the handlebars in a spasm with each downstroke. Learn not to do this. Let the legs do the work! In all of this, observe others and their faults as I have done, as well as riders who have either naturally come to good practice or been coached. When you see it in others it is easier to be motivated to change.

IN BRIEF

Learning a smooth pedalling action takes lots of time and sometimes continual adjustment to perfect, but the value in taking the time and effort to produce a technically efficient pedal stroke will lead to improved performance and you will look a classy rider.

- Think about the detail of the pedal stroke at every point in the circumference of the pedalling action
- Study your position on your bike in relation to engagement with the pedal
- Avoid erratic body movement while pedalling, keep upper torso still where possible and focus on the pedal action in relation to feet, ankles and legs
- Think about the pedal stroke, dead spots and where you can get extra from that stroke

10

Stretching

Stretching and suppleness are essential if you are to fulfil your potential as a cyclist. Stretching is what we do, and suppleness is what we gain from it. This is an aspect of performance maximisation that I consider to be the most overlooked by the average club rider. Even those that I have encouraged to do more stretching for the good of their overall performance have rarely continued for a sustained period. Their rationale appears to be that if they are flexible enough to perform the pedalling action then why bother being more flexible still.

This thinking is completely wrong since the ability to perform the pedalling stroke is not included in any part of the benefits that I will explain. It is also wrong in that it makes no difference to the pedalling stroke that they are performing currently, but makes a huge difference to the fluidity and efficiency of the pedalling stroke that they ought to be using (I covered this in the chapter on pedalling). A lot of people are also put off by the confusing array of stretches out there and by the idea that time spent on an inert action on the floor could be better used to do more cycling or just resting. For a lot of people, sporting or not, stretching is simply an alien activity that they have never taken seriously.

I realise that it is most likely that readers of this book will take on some parts of it and leave others. It is unfortunate that only those who believe in stretching can appreciate its importance and those that don't will never notice the difference. Let me give you an example from my own experience. I stretch every day and know my own suppleness limits intimately.

After I do a huge session on the bike and especially strength training, I find I cannot achieve the same flexibility that I can usually achieve. My suppleness is such that even a large drop-off from my normal level still leaves me suppler than the average cyclist. Now suppose I was the average cyclist, then this drop-off would impinge on my ability to pedal freely. The average cyclist never notices this because they don't stretch. The point I make is that stretching is vitally important, and it is not yoga or some strange new world of complicated body contortion. In my whole career I did a routine of just four stretches and trust me, if I had not, I would never have been the rider I was. You would never accept having a stiff bottom bracket so don't accept having a stiff body! The benefits are remarkable when you consider also that it has been shown that a suppleness programme reduces sports injuries considerably.

The benefits of stretching are more than just how freely your legs go round. The free movement of your joints is enhanced by forcing them past the position that normal life and cycling needs. Think of it as a bit like a hinge that has been opening only part of the way. Working it back and forth makes it work more freely altogether. Then there is the benefit to the muscles. The muscles are made of long cells that run across each other a bit like two brushes stuck together. When we ride, these cells pull together through a complicated energy system that it is not necessary to explain here. What you need to know is that the muscles can only contract, they cannot extend themselves. This only happens by the force of opposing muscles. When our muscles are tired then the contraction and extension process is diminished. When we do our stretching routine we pull the cells apart, like pulling the brushes apart, in a way that would not happen normally by lying about in recovery with tired bodies.

The benefit of doing this is that we get our muscles moving again. In the act of doing this we stimulate the flow of blood and help the removal of lactic acid. We also facilitate the flow of nutrients to the muscle. Bearing in mind that a large part of any muscle is engaged in the storage and utilisation of glycogen (a form of starch that powers the muscle) then it is clear that getting the muscle moving through stretching is important in re-energising the muscle in a way that massage alone cannot achieve.

Then there are the tendons and ligaments that transfer the force and power of the muscle as it contracts. A regular and continuous programme of stretching will help these tendons and ligaments work more efficiently. Tendons and ligaments that are only used for general life can be too short for good flexibility, but over a period of time they can be made the right length for an efficient pedalling machine.

There are four basic stretches that I would advise you do. Before describing them I need to impart a very important point. Do not lunge or bounce while doing a stretch since this is a shortcut to injury and the benefits are limited anyway.

The first stretch is the humble hamstring stretch where you lie on the floor and try to touch your toes with your legs kept straight. You can do this one standing up but I find it more comfortable and sustainable as a

STRETCH

— complete the full cycle —

floor exercise. You will feel this in the back of your legs. Do not be overly alarmed if you can't touch your toes at the start. The important thing is that you have your starting point, and it is also worth noting that since upper body morphology varies from person to person then it is not the proximity of fingers to toes that matters but the angle of the body in relation to the floor. The important thing is to pull your shoulders as close to the knee as possible.

The second stretch is a standing one where you balance on one foot with leg and body straight. Keeping knees together bend the other leg and grab the top of your foot and pull it towards your buttock. You will feel the stretch across the front of the thigh. Alternate legs, of course, and if you find it difficult to balance then try focusing on one point ahead of you. The most important factor is maintaining a straight posture and keeping knees side by side.

The third stretch is best done lying on your back. Keeping a straight posture, pull one leg towards your chest by clasping your hands over the front of the knee. Alternate the legs but be sure to keep the 'resting' leg straight.

The fourth stretch involves squatting down and using the body's own weight. From a standing start, place your feet at 90° with the heels touching. If you squat down so that your knees are either side of you and relax your muscles, then you can let your body weight do the stretch for you. The best policy is to put your arms out in front of you in the tri-bar position. If you do this correctly, you should be resting purely on the balls of your feet.

Ideally, the best way to get started is to rotate between these four stretches, doing perhaps 30 seconds on each one. The best time of the day is evening when the body is naturally suppler from the movement throughout the day. The whole stretching process should not last more than 10 or 15 minutes and it should not be a chore to do it. Once you are up and going you will probably find it quite relaxing and over the course of time you will notice quite a bit of difference in how flexible you are with each exercise.

The other thing people ask me about is how much of this you should do in the process of warming up before a race. Counter to established thinking, my own opinion is that you should do very little of it beforehand and if you do then it should be very light and only after doing a bit of pedalling about to loosen the muscles and increase blood flow. Suppleness is something that is gained progressively and once you start getting more flexible then you are not going to wake up and it's all gone. Few people get straight out of bed feeling brand new and ready to take the start line, so don't force your body to be as supple as it was the evening before by going straight to a stretching routine.

The last word on all of this is that gaining this suppleness is a lot more work than maintaining it. Persevere with it and the accumulation of tiny gains makes a real difference. To be honest, maintaining the suppleness I had in my racing career would take as little as five minutes – but only if I stuck to the schedule every night!

IN BRIEF

Suppleness is what we gain from stretching, and a supple body will react faster, perform better and recover from injury quicker than a non-supple body. The suppleness needed for a cyclist can be achieved in a short daily session that is not too demanding and will provide lasting benefits.

- A regular stretching programme will help tendons and ligaments work more efficiently
- You would never accept having a stiff bottom bracket so don't accept having a stiff body
- It is best to stretch when the body is warmed up, and remember, don't rush a cold body into exaggerated stretch positions as this can lead to injury

11

The time trial

Time-trialling, the timed solo effort over a set distance, is known as the race of truth since it is seen as the ultimate test of pure physical ability – how hard a rider can pedal relating directly to how quickly they can complete the distance. This is a simplistic view, implying that few other factors have any influence other than the riders' physical fitness. The true situation is quite different and the science, physics and tactics are actually quite complex.

Major factors in the final outcome are already in place before the rider even starts, such as bike set-up and positioning as well as physical and tactical preparation. Choice of equipment is clearly important but very often too much time, energy and resources are expended on this aspect of the sport to the detriment of other equally important issues. The difference between a good aerodynamic modern TT frame and top-of-the-range in terms of performance is remarkably small and the same can be said of wheels and other pieces of equipment. There really is no point in putting yourself under pressure to get the most expensive equipment when mid-range items possess almost the same physical characteristics. It is worth spending a little more to get carbon-soled shoes, as previously mentioned, and a good quality aero helmet that fits well. Shoe covers are a must since it is an established fact that they reduce the aerodynamic drag. Admittedly, the overall difference is tiny, but a gain is a gain. There is one thing to consider as a matter of practicality, which is whether to use carbon wheels or those that have an alloy rim. I say this on the grounds that it is not good to train on your TT machine, riding your best full-carbon wheels, in terms of wear, damage and punctures. It is better to have training wheels with more robust tyres, but the problem lies in the fact that carbon rims require carbon-specific brake blocks and changing to alloy rims for training requires changing brake blocks each time. So either you decide to put up with the time it takes and inconvenience to change brake blocks or you decide from the start that you buy all-carbon race and training wheels or all-alloy. It is a point to consider when faced with a pair of very tempting 'bling' wheels in a shop.

success or otherwise on the day is largely dictated by the build-up and preparation that preceded it

A point to bear in mind is the entire gearing issue. How many cogs in the rear, what ratios, what front ring sizes, single chainring or double? The best way to deal with best set-up is to first ask: what type of events will I be concentrating on and what extremes of gearing will I need? The majority of TTs in the UK are relatively flat-course, standard-distance events, in which case a single chainring is sufficient with a close ratio cluster in the rear. For such events it is worth having a larger than standard front ring (58-tooth is available) for better chain-line and efficiency. It is a good idea to try and get a rear cassette set that is close ratio in the first seven or eight with wider jumps on the last two or three for warming-up or unexpected gradients.

Ironically, in flat events like these, the weight factor has little effect on performance and the extra chainring and lever would make little difference. On the other hand, hilly TTs and many triathlon events have a lot more elevation to overcome, but the weight of a double chainring is necessary for the sake of gearing. From my own perspective of following a regime of suppleness I have been happy to ride hilly or even mountainous events (Isle of Man TT for example) on a single ring with wide ratio cassette since suppleness allows a wider range of pedal rate variation. Even with a double ring there is an advantage in going wider ratio since it means that not only can you get the amount of gear shift you really need in one click but you can find a gear that works on a climb while still using the large chainring. Wide ratio means that each gear changes a considerable amount with each click. This is hugely important since using the rear cassette one gear at a time maintains rhythm whereas changing to a small chainring disrupts everything because the jump is too big, and then you have to change up a gear or three in the rear if you are using close ratio. In short, close ratio is good for just one type of TT – relatively flat set-distance events.

I have to mention the use of fixed-wheel machines. There are definite advantages and disadvantages in opting for this set-up. Constancy of pace and targeting an effort on tough parts are the benefits as well, of course, as the fact there is less bike and fewer components obstructing airflow. The chain efficiency is also the most efficient that can be achieved. There is the psychological factor that there is no other gear to turn to so when the going gets tough there is no 'lazy level' to fall back on so the mind focuses instead on getting the gear you have turning well. Then there is the downside, which I have been the victim of on several occasions. If it is either blowing a near gale or the course is hillier than expected – or worse still both – then the fixed wheel becomes a huge disadvantage simply because most of the race is spent either grossly over-geared or under-geared and you maintain almost no rhythm at all.

There is a best solution policy to consider. The first priority is to have a geared bike. After that if you have resources and fancy a new worthwhile sideline then it is not a bad idea to put together a fixed machine. When you go to events or training rides then you have the choice of what bike to use. Riding fixed can help change the way that you tackle a TT even if you are switching to gears. I will come back to this later in regard to tactics.

In equipment terms the choice of tyres is very important and can make a big enough difference to matter. In all events and circumstances I would *never* recommend the narrowest tyres. In fact I always go for the widest edition of any race tyre purely on the basis that it reduces the chance of tyre and wheel damage and provides a reduction in the rolling resistance. The big question has to be how light shall I go and how much does the race in question matter compared to the extra risk of puncturing? The lighter the tyre the faster it will roll but the easier it will puncture since the rubber is thinner. Personally, if it is the big day, I always risk the lightest I can get away with. There is also a myth that pumping your tyres to the highest pressure that they can withstand will produce the best performance. A pressure of 130 to 150 psi (9 to 10 bar) is as much as necessary. Beyond this is disadvantageous in terms of deformation on the road surface, cornering and increased puncture risk.

Another piece of kit to look at is the skinsuit. It is good to have a choice of either long or short sleeve to choose from depending on the temperature and weather conditions. Most riders are members of clubs and have to buy from the club stock, but if it comes to reordering then I strongly recommend trying to get suits that zip up the back on the grounds that they are more aerodynamic and comfortable by the fact there is no crinkle of compressed zip in the riding position. I have to mention to women riders that the all-important last pee is not so easy – especially if your number is attached already. It is also worth noting that extra aerodynamic fabric has been developed that makes a real difference, but I have not been able to find out much about it despite enquiry. This is still the preserve of secretive federations, but asking the question at the point of ordering might be worth a shot.

The question of what and how much to wear in the event is one that can be answered beforehand with the benefit of modern accurate weather forecasting. Knowing the time of your start you can normally find out pretty much exactly what to expect during your ride. The important factors are if it will be wet and what the temperature is forecast to be. Most riders race in scant clothing that they would never dream of wearing in the same conditions in a training session. In the UK we live in a temperate climate, and since most TT events take place early in the day then it is safe to say that more often than not there will be cool conditions. A good investment is a pair of lightweight leg warmers and I will set a point for their use at anything under 10°C. This would be combined with long sleeve skinsuit and cotton undergarment.

get your race machine ready and set about the business of focusing and warm-up

A common practice for cold conditions is to use creams and potions with weird names implying heat. These are worse than useless! Much worse. These are in fact irritants in a cream form, and the reason they are so bad is that although they give the feeling of warmth because of the irritation they cause on the surface of the skin, they generate almost no warmth what-so-ever. They provide almost no insulating effect either. This is not the worst of it though. Because of the irritant effect warm blood is drawn nearer to the surface and the net result is that the core temperature lowers in genuinely cold conditions even though the victim of this age-old trade feels warm at the moment. Don't be taken in by the organic and natural labels either – opium, cocaine and shark attacks get those big green ticks as well. Lycra longs is the answer to cool conditions.

The success or otherwise on the day is largely dictated by the build-up and preparation that preceded it. Rewinding four days, let's say your event is Sunday morning and this is Wednesday. Firstly, you have to prioritise the event and decide whether to taper down for total readiness or whether to follow your incremental plan of improvement. It's a straight choice, either I get another training ride in and risk being slightly jaded or I turn my legs over and ride from a position of total recovery? Let me put it in perspective. If it is not a championship or major personal best opportunity, then train. It has to be said that if it is neither of these, then you have to think clearly about what there is to gain from taking part at all, in terms of consistent improvement to achieve the goals that do matter to you.

The other point to take into consideration when it comes to tapering down to an event is the time of day. A lot of riders have been caught out by thinking that riding an evening event on the Thursday before a championship event on the Sunday will be fine. Well, the championship event is not three days away, it is two and a half days away and that will have a huge difference.

tiny

+ gains +

make a real difference

Whatever your decision is then the morning of the event you have whatever potential you have and building up to the moment of being on the start list is crucial to bringing out your best possible performance.

When you get up on the morning of your event then the distance you have to ride has a large bearing on what you eat and drink. For me, early-start events did not fit naturally into my biological rhythm, and I made a point of getting up earlier than I had to in order to kick-start the bodily function process so that I could be in the physiological equivalent of mid-morning by the time I made my early start. The most important thing in my mind was that I had to visit the toilet before I set off, knowing that I always went in the morning as my norm. Getting up four hours before your start time is good practice and at least two hours before you need to travel is essential. You need to get your body into the mode of normal morning routine earlier than it is used to in order to be fully in awake and ready mode by the time of your race start. It is important to be able to go to the toilet before you set off not only for physical reasons but also because you do not want to be at your event thinking that you will need to go to the toilet before you start, especially as facilities at events are usually very busy. A good way of promoting a bowel movement is having a strong cup of peppermint tea when you first get up.

How much and what you eat depends on the length of your event. If it will last no more than two hours, there is no need to gorge yourself and eating on the light side is the best plan since providing you have been training to maximise your glycogen stores then energy for your ride will be there already. The best morning food is bland things such as toast or cereal. More important is the intake of fluids. Avoid drinks that have high sugar content like commercially available energy drinks. These will only raise your blood sugar level which will trigger an insulin rush leaving you drained and less motivated. Take fibre-rich carbohydrate food with you and plenty of water. Wholegrain bread with a scrape of jam or marmalade is ideal since the mix of sugar, long-chain carbohydrate and fibre provides a good source of energy without a sugar spike provided you learn to nibble at it and don't eat a pile of it at once. If you have been training on this system, then you will have the confidence to know that the energy you need is within you already. If your event is longer, then there is a need for fuelling for the ride. The most important thing is water along with your choice of food (see Chapter 12) that you have used in training. Use energy drinks if you have been doing OK with them in training but do not be tempted to overdo the scoops since over-strong solution is worse than none at all. Bear in mind that the actual calories are much less than you may think. Two half-litre bottles will contain enough energy to fuel about 12–15 minutes of actual riding so real food is also needed.

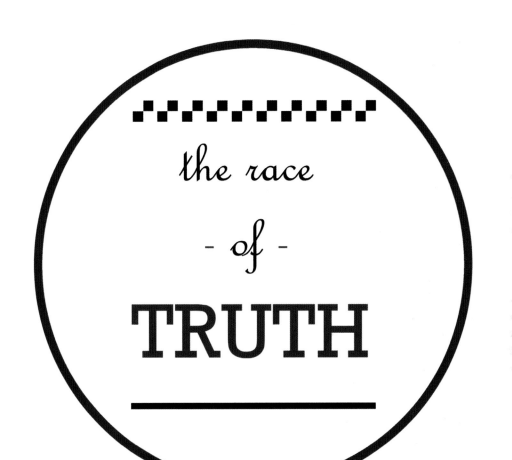

the race

- of -

TRUTH

a fundamental truth about time-trialling is that they are not won by going fast but by *not going slow*

At the event you need to deal with signing on and getting changed quickly. Get your race machine ready and set about the business of focusing and warm-up. The ideal thing if the weather is dry is to ride out part of the course to assess the wind direction and strength. An important aspect of doing your best ride is knowing the terrain of the course. This is not always possible with constraints of work and other commitments, but at best you can drive down part of the route on the way to the event. If this is your major event of the season, then ride round the course the evening before and make a mental note of the turns and undulations. If you want to take it very seriously – and we do – then record the course on a helmet-mounted camera and play back on your laptop. Note wind direction and check weather forecast. How much water to drink in the run up to the starting point depends on the distance of the event and weather conditions. For a 10-mile TT, prepare as you would for a turbo session. For 25-mile TTs, the best part of a bottle of water just before the line is enough, but if the weather is very hot then having more liquid halfway through is a good plan. For 50-mile events at least one large water bottle is essential as well as downing as much as you comfortably can with minutes to spare.

As you warm up, visualise the places that will be the most challenging in terms of maintaining speed because of wind direction and gradient. A fundamental truth about time-trialling is that they are not won by going fast but by *not going slow*! An important factor, vital even, when looking at the course is to assess where you can stop for at least one pee before the start since hydration is so important and not even being slightly ready on the line is essential to good physical and psychological readiness.

It is a good thing to know in advance if you have a tailwind or headwind or otherwise in the outer leg of a time trial since this dictates the initial intensity of your effort. This has a bearing on the importance and intensity of your warm-up effort on the turbo. A tailwind start means that your first few miles will have to be less than maximal followed by all-out effort into the headwind finish, which means the first part although intense is an extension of the warm-up itself. A headwind start is a different matter. A full and quite rigorous warm-up is needed since a full-on effort will be needed from the gun. Visualising what you must do and where to do it against what conditions ahead of the event is a way to maximise your velocity under scientific and mathematical principles.

Riding at a steady output of power over a course that varies in wind direction and gradient will always lose out to riding selectively hard and

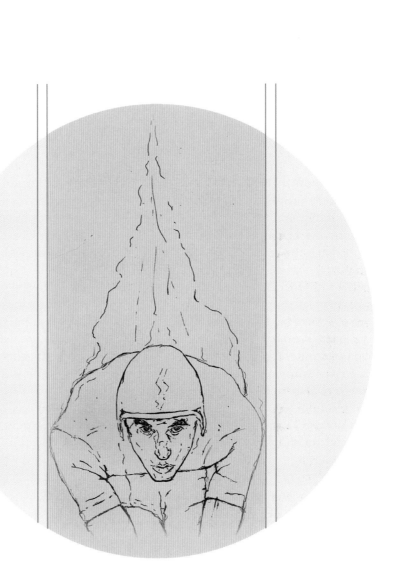

easier in order to not go slow. This is basic maths and physics, but the bottom line is that the clever rider using the same calories overall but using them to maintain pace on the hard bits and ticking along on the easier sections will go considerably faster over the distance. This takes confidence and experience. Fixed-wheel riding forces you to ride like this, and if you can gain an insight from it then you can apply this at all times, even if you are on gears at the time. In the real world of competition you should be looking ahead to the next tough part of the course and back off a fraction in the run-up to that section, in order to go harder than a sustainable effort on the harder section. How much you adjust your effort depends on that. The rule is simple: time trials are won not by going fast but by not going slow.

In terms of physics, there is the object being propelled forward by a force (force on rear tyre against the road) opposed by the force of resistance, which is primarily air resistance, combined with a much smaller resistance from tyre deformation. Assuming that full training, ride technique and breathing control have been adopted then the only end of the equation, the only way of changing the equilibrium, is to reduce resistance. The largest part of that resistance is aerodynamic drag, and the fact that we are riding the thinnest rubber we dare, then the only thing to focus on in the machine set-up stage is to minimise aerodynamic drag.

A good start is to see if you can reduce the height of your elbow pads or to become suppler and perhaps lose some weight as a result of diet control. The most important factor to reduce drag is narrowing the elbows as much as possible. Some bar systems, expensive as they are, do not allow any serious adjustment. In terms of velocity it is better to have a cheap heavy bar set-up that allows you to get your elbows as close as you can comfortably than carry on with snazzy carbon one-piece aero bars. Getting the elbows 'narrow' out on the road is the number one priority.

OK, you are not totally convinced. Wave your hand about. Feel the thick air waft between your fingers. We live in a thick soup that is the lower atmosphere. We are like gold fish that do not know they are swimming in water. Feel that air, that gaseous soup. It's not about weight – it's about cutting through that soup as efficiently as possible. That is the majority of rider's limitations in almost all disciplines. If you can get a real sense of that then you can get a better appreciation of positioning and the suppleness needed to make the best of it

There are things you can do during your ride that will help facilitate the passage of atmospheric soup more easily. The first thing is to be able to use the rolling riding style I described earlier, but on the road a major focal point to make it cohesive and fluid is to keep your head in the same line at all times. This enables you to slightly lower your torso since the knees are slightly wide of the chest cavity at each stroke. Another small advantage in cutting through the air is to learn the goose-neck technique of letting your head drop while keeping the same inclination. Most of the time in time-trialling, the defining attribute to minimising aerodynamic drag is how bent over a rider can be yet still pedal with full power. Deliberately letting the head drop a little takes a bit of height off what is normally the highest point of the rider and reduces the frontal area. This can be practised on the turbo. Take care not to over-tighten your shoes, as unhindered ankle movement will help in achieving a smooth pedal action while in your aero position. The bottom line is an unavoidable fact. How fast you go in a flat time trial is mostly governed by how aero you can maintain your body position while still producing a high output of power.

When you finally get to the start line you have to be clear in your mind that you will not make the mistake that most riders do most of the time. Setting off at a pace that is not sustainable is easily done, and it takes a lot of confidence not to. Even if it is a headwind start and you know that you have to hit it hard, it is still essential to have pace control, especially in the first two or three miles. Consider the single pace turbo sessions and how the first five minutes or so seem easy yet in the end you are hanging on to hold the pace. It is better to risk setting off too slowly than go too hard and condemn yourself to a diminishing ride. You will always lose more in the end than anything you gained from an unsustainable start. Use the first part instead to find your rhythm, pedal action and breath control. These are the things that will set you up for your best ride.

IN BRIEF

Careful preparation is vital to a successful time trial, care in training, bike set-up and positioning. Think of the air as a sticky soup through which it is necessary to propel yourself and your body. Every effort to reduce frontal air resistance will have a benefit (within the rules of the sport of course). Please bear in mind that a fundamental truth about time-trialling is that they are not won by going fast but by *not going slow*.

- The more information you can compile about a time trial the better; the route, the elevations and descents and the weather can all determine your ability to perform to your potential
- Ensure you arrive at the event with your equipment and gear in perfect order
- Find your rhythm as early as possible and don't overcook your effort in the outward section of the effort; time your effort to maximise output over the duration of the event

Nutrition and diet

Nutrition is an aspect of preparation that is often neglected. We need to be as obsessive with our nutrition planning as we are with our training plan, or bike set-up. Bear in mind the old saying, 'you are what you eat'. It is more applicable to athletes than to the ordinary citizen. In the space of a year the majority of our bodies will be gone and replaced by new and different atoms and molecules. Our bodies are in a constant state of flux with current material being discharged and replaced in a constant process of renewal; even our bones are not permanent. The only renewal source for all of this bodily material is harnessed from what we consume. The food we eat is literally the making of us.

Dietary information and advice can be terribly confusing especially when scientific findings seem to be contradictory, swinging from one finding to the next, often with supposed scientific findings reversed soon after they have been trumpeted as an important breakthrough! A good example is the case of eggs, first they were good for you, then they were not because of cholesterol, and at this time they are known to actually help reduce cholesterol and contain vital vitamins as well as the benefits of quality proteins – apparently. I always thought this was the case anyway and never stopped eating them. A pertinent point that never gets mentioned in scientific studies is that aerobic endurance athletes, like cyclists, have a much higher metabolism than the subjects used in these studies. This means that cyclists' bodies also have a more efficient mechanism of uptaking and disposing of good and bad substances. What may be bad for inactive people is not necessarily the case for us. Scientific advice given in mainstream media is neither tested on us nor relevant to us as far as mainstream foods are concerned.

There is also the question of who gives advice and why? It is good to ask the age-old question that has been good since Roman times: 'qui bono?', translated as 'who benefits?' It is a good question to ask when any product is advised and financial transaction is involved, but in the field of nutrition there has been a trend towards refined foods such as protein, carbohydrate and vitamins that are more expensive than their real-food counterparts. Advocating real food has no financial gain.

In the real world of coming home from work and trying to fit in training and riding with social commitments, there is no point in being obsessive and fussy about it: eat family meals just the same. The secret is to be selective about what parts of prepared meals you want to consume in moderation and deciding on which parts you choose to have extra helpings of. Let's face it, we are not living in a space station so we can eat real food that contains *all* of the nutrients and calories that we need. What we do need to do is moderate our intake of foods that we know are high in bad substances like saturated fat and salt and concentrate on ones that are healthier. In the field of general health and nutrition there is no need for supplements of any kind. The thing to be aware of is that supplements are often refined products derived from real food in the first instance. The nature of refining is that the bulk of other stuff has to be removed so that a purified version of a particular nutrient, such as protein, remains. In a lot of cases the natural food contains substances that act in conjunction with others to aid its digestion and uptake. This is most common in the case of vitamins where these have molecules called coenzymes coexisting in the natural food product that are vital to the uptake and assimilation of the vitamin. There is also the fact that the human body can only process and store a certain amount of most types of vitamin and mineral. Consuming excessive amounts in the form of supplements can actually have a negative effect on your body since the liver and kidneys have to work hard to process and eliminate them from your system. All the nutrition you will ever need is contained in the real food of a balanced diet. Our bodies and our digestive system have evolved to deal with a diet of real food and real vegetables and as omnivores to digest meat and fish as well.

As far as the balanced diet goes the advice that your grandma would give is generally a good rule to follow, except that we need to be mindful to dramatically cut down on the salt contained in an old-fashioned diet as well as saturated fat. In the modern world where a lot of foodstuffs are also refined and processed this is not as easy as it sounds. A bit of forward planning and selective shopping is required – as well as looking at labels and learning to know what figures actually mean. A few changes in the way we prepare food are also advisable.

A lot of foods that seem low in salt or fat can actually be quite unhealthy. A good example is canned soup. This commonly has a salt content of 0.6g per 100g but when you consider the can contains 400g then this is a total salt value of 2.4g. The problem is that in comparison to the other nutrients this is a very high percentage of salt indeed. The can of vegetable soup I have in front of me only contains 6g of protein and 152 calories and is made up of in excess of 90 per cent water, so the dry weight of that food is over 16 per cent salt. When you consider that the current government target is not to exceed 6g per day then you can see that a tin of soup with two slices of bread can exceed over half this quota. That 6g target is still way in excess of actual bodily need. Biologically, we require little over 1g a day to retain good health. Avoiding salt is difficult and confusing since labels rarely give dry weight percentages. The problem with excessive sodium intake from standard salt is that it affects us adversely at a cellular level by changing the osmotic balance. This is the process that causes slugs to disintegrate due to pressure on the cell wall. Although not so destructive to humans, our cells have to work hard to resist this potent effect and the ability of our cells to exchange other molecules through the membrane is impaired by it. Anything over 2g or 3g a day can be considered mild poisoning. The problem with all this is that looking at labels can take an age and the information displayed can be erratic. The answer is to get to know the best foods at your local shop and avoid the worst excesses. While looking at labels on food I have come across a standard size tin of macaroni and cheese containing 6g of salt – the government health limit for consumption during a day. The best solution is to cook a lot of your food from scratch with basic and wholesome ingredients. This sounds like a mammoth task yet it need not be the case. The secret is to make use of efficiency of scale. It is almost as quick to prepare a huge pot of soup as enough for just one day. This is also true for other foods like low-fat and low-salt curries, chillies and spaghetti bolognaise. Making your own bread with low salt content is also easy, and all of these foods can be bagged or put into containers and frozen for quick ready meals. When it comes to soup making, stock cubes should be avoided because of their ridiculously high salt content. Use spices and herbs to flavour your soup instead.

Curries, chillies and 'spagbol' can all be made using sieved tomatoes as a base rather than saltier and higher fat pre-prepared jars of sauce. A big advantage is that you can drain off a lot of the fat from even such as lean mince in the first stage of cooking. I would usually use wholegrain rice and spaghetti as well and premix each portion before freezing so that a complete meal comes out of the microwave. With all of these meals I would recommend having a good portion of vegetables as a side serving. The best and easiest way of preparing this is simply taking broccoli, carrots and perhaps mixed vegetables and microwaving then for four to five minutes in a covered bowl. Frozen vegetables are not only easy but are actually nutritionally better than fresh produce as well as being substantially cheaper, home-grown vegetables aside. Vegetables start to degrade and lose their vitamin content as soon as they are picked, and this is why you should never take veggies from the reduced isle no matter how cheap they are. Fresh vegetables can never be truly fresh from a supermarket since there is transport time combined with shelf time. Real fresh is picked from your garden or allotment, the best option if not always the most practical, but to be honest frozen is good enough.

I have held back from telling you exactly what to eat at what time every day. That would be regimented and boring. The important points to remember are to cut out or reduce salt intake and saturated fat wherever possible and to have potatoes and wholegrain rice and wholewheat pasta as a carbohydrate base as much as possible.

It is a fact of being an aerobic athlete that you need to consume more calories simply because you burn off a lot of energy in training. A good way to address the calorie deficit is to snack on fruit like apples and bananas and eating good quality cereal with skimmed or semi-skimmed milk. Again it is important to look at the salt, sugar and fat content of these. Most cereals are processed and are high in both salt and sugar. The sugar content is not good since it will cause a sugar spike and insulin rush that will upset the equilibrium of your body. The best ones are either wheat that is shredded and has nothing but wheat in it or wheat bisks. Ironically, the cheaper brands of wheat bisks have less processing and less salt added. The best cereal of all though is porridge. You can make this with no salt or very little, but the downside is the time it takes to make.

Cereals and especially porridge have high protein content but it is important to realise that protein is a generic name for a class of molecule that varies widely in shape, size and molecular make-up. Protein can be made up of a variety of what are called amino acids. There are twenty of these that we require, and our bodies can synthesise eleven of them from other nutrients. Nine are known as essential amino acids and we need them to be part of our diet in order to maintain and rebuild our body structure. A combination of both plant and animal-based protein (including fish and dairy) will give us all the building blocks our bodies need. Sardines are one of the best sources of protein and omega-3 oils. (For those who follow vegetarian or vegan diets then careful dietary planning is needed to ensure adequate protein consumption.)

The good thing about sardines is that they are far down the food chain so don't build up a store of toxins from other fish the way, for instance, tuna does. Also, gram for gram they are more nutritious than salmon or tuna. A good tip is to mush them with a squirt of tomato sauce. Buying them in olive oil is the best bet, and try and use a lot of the oil with the mix since the olive oil and fish oil are both good fats to have. Not all fat is bad.

Another point to mention is that if we are living, training and eating in a social environment, and other people around you will want to eat nice stuff

like cakes and puddings. It is hard to resist these since we are human and these foods are really tempting, and also we don't always want to seem like obsessive spoilsports so the best policy is to eat and enjoy but in moderation with small portions. Soft drink is another area to look at since what may seem like a healthy choice is far from it. It is important to be wary of both fruit juices, such as apple and orange, and smoothies. Pure orange juice contains 9 per cent sugar and little else of value other than vitamin C (ascorbic acid), incidentally, also contained in eggs! A better choice is diluting juice or 'no added sugar' blackcurrant juice or herbal tea, or even low calorie cola.

Going out socially and eating a meal with friends is a time when we have no real control over what is on the menu. My take on it is that generally all the meals will be salty and fatty, but since it is not a nightly occurrence and you are out to enjoy yourself then just eat what you want. Sometimes we think we can do the right thing and order what seems like the healthy option. There are two problems with this. Firstly, this is not what you would order and enjoy if you were not being conscientious of diet, and secondly, the healthy option rarely is much healthier than the choice you would have made. A good example of this is Caesar salad. This has more calories, salt and fat than most other options, and lettuce has so much less vitamin content than other vegetables that you would have been better off ordering steak pie and piling into the vegetables and whole potatoes that come with it. More than anything you would enjoy it more and general satisfaction and happiness in life are important in the long term for sustained motivation. There are limits though, especially if you are riding the next day. Some carry-out foods have been known to contain in excess of 20g of salt in a single meal. When you consider that 50g can be a fatal dose then it is clear to see why a bit of selectivity could make a difference to how you feel.

A policy of mine when it comes to eating out is to break away from the strictness of my diet for a while. When it comes to starters, I always ask for sticky toffee pudding or whatever else takes my fancy from the sweet menu. There are two very good reasons behind this, the first being that most non-athletes do not burn up enough calories to be able to consume both starter and sweet with the result that sweet gets abandoned after main, so I go for exactly what I want in my culinary blowout. Secondly, the sweet is usually healthier than the starter in terms of salt and fat content and a whole lot more enjoyable.

If I have to cover every aspect of consumption, then alcohol intake must be included. The truth is that there have been many cases of great rides being achieved on the back of alcohol consumption that could only be accurately described as over-consumption. Indeed I have done this on a few occasions myself. The truth, though, is that they were done despite the alcohol and not because of the alcohol. Alcohol contains empty calories and there can only be two benefits from consuming it. One, that we feel relaxed and chill out a bit more and that this is good for the morale after a sustained period of dedication. The other is that we can sleep well after a few drinks. The problem with the societal timetable is that social events tend to take place on Friday and Saturday evening and races take place on Saturday and Sunday mornings. A compromise has to be made, and a good idea in terms of long-term systematic improvement while keeping up a social life in the on-season is not to race every weekend. As much as anything drink moderately. A point of real importance to clear up in the general dietary policy is the idea that you have to load your consumption in the early part of every day and eat very lightly in the evening. This idea has become standard advice without substantive scientific evidence. The theory is that eating in the early part of the day will result in nutrients being used to enhance the physical changes needed for athletic improvement whereas eating in the evening will only lead to those nutrients being converted into fat to be stored in the adipose cells (fat-storing cells).

In my experience it is best to eat lightly in the morning and early day in order that a good size evening and pre-bed meal can be consumed. The fact of the matter is that during waking hours the body can only do its best to limit breaking down. In sleep, the brain, the muscles and the immune system all regenerate in a way that is not possible during waking hours. Having a hearty supper will not only provide the nutrients and calories needed for revitalisation, but more than anything it is a good basis for a sound sleep. Eating and sleeping is the way to go.

To sum up the eating plan for a healthy athletic diet, you should look at what is actually in your food on a comparative basis of what is good against what is bad. Looking at labels and comparing the salt content and fat content against the total food and water content is a good start. Looking at the carbohydrate content and at the information that depicts salt and sugar content is essential. More than anything follow your conscious instinct since we generally have an idea of foods that are good and those that are not. Although we feel little different in the moment, the long-term effect on our well-being and progress physically as aerobic athletes is determined by the quality of what we eat or don't eat.

When it comes to fuelling a competitive ride or a sportive then two factors come into play. One is the level of nutrition and stored energy the body has on the start line by means of general good eating as part of any training and eating plan. An important point to make is that if you eat a hearty meal before going to bed then this will be a natural thing for your body on the eve of an event. The second is if you eat and drink before and during the ride itself. You should not underestimate the importance of the first point in that a lot of athletes who buy into this idea of going to bed almost hungry to avoid feeding the fat stores, suddenly want to eat carbohydrate (usually not wholegrain) on the evening priot to an event. If you are training your glycogen storage system as described in previous chapters and you have allowed yourself good recovery time and a good diet, then where exactly is this extra carbohydrate going to be stored? The answer is that it can only be converted to fat or hurried through your digestive system by your body. The only benefit of stuffing yourself with processed low-fibre pasta is when you are riding a multi-stage event and you are trying to restock your glycogen system for the next day. Eating a load of standard pasta, the type that is the usual fare at pre-event pasta parties is equivalent to working your way through a bag of white flour. This can cause a sugar spike in your bloodstream that requires insulin from the liver to control. The resulting dip in sugar level will be addressed partly from glycogen stores you already have.

The best plan is to follow the diet that you are used to on the eve of an event, and on the eve of a long sportive it is best policy to take your own meal with you. The best food is probably wholegrain cereal with skimmed milk or wholegrain sandwiches with meat or cheese filling (vegans or those following special diets will need to identify the appropriate foodstuff for that particular diet). At this point there is no point in worrying about veggies or vitamins – these are the things that you already have in your system from good eating as explained earlier. If your event is short or medium length, then the same rule applies: eat well and sleep well! The only variation is what you eat and drink on the morning of the event.

If, for example, the event is a ten-mile time trial then on the morning of your event you will eat very lightly. A couple of slices of toast will do and nibbling lightly on a banana or jam sandwich until the start line while being mindful of hydration. This would hold true also of a 25 miler. If the event is 50 miles or more, then a more substantial breakfast will be desirable, but stuffing yourself will only work against you and the energy gap has to be filled with calories consumed during the event.

There are a vast array of products on sale aimed at fuelling your ride as well as supplements and post-training recovery drinks. It is easy to be drawn to the conclusion that you must have these products if you are to avoid being disadvantaged. Nothing could be further from the truth. As far as post-training recovery goes then nothing is going to be better than a well-prepared balanced meal. My usual is sardines mashed on wholemeal toast with a veggie side serving, but it can be any meal of choice. A good habit is to get your meal ready for immediate reheat and consumption as soon as you return from your event or training.

As far as fuelling the ride itself there are two main areas to look at. One is what can be added to water and the other is what will be eaten. When it comes to energy drinks it has to be pointed out that at normal concentration

a standard half-litre bottle will contain about 110 calories. During a race long enough to require feeding, an average rider at full tilt will be expending about 1300 calories or more an hour.

In order to balance intake of energy the rider would have to consume a whole water bottle every five minutes for the entire event. Let's not dismiss energy drinks out of hand since some input is better than none, provided it does not cause stomach or digestion problems. I mention this because energy drinks and gels fall into the same category in that neither of them is chewed or stimulate salivation, which is the first stage of enzyme release and digestion. Bypassing this first stage can cause discomfort for a number of people so my advice is to never ever try something new in an event and always test things first in training rides that mimic the race situation.

It is important to note that total balance of energy in and energy out is not essential since most trained and recovered athletes will have useful glycogen stores of 2000–4000 calories to draw on as well as a relatively small but constant trickle of energy from fat conversion and not forgetting of course the food being digested in the stomach at the start. Nonetheless, on a long ride there is an energy gap that needs bridging, and since the body is 47 per cent efficient, the same amount again is lost as heat. Clearly, on a long ride actual food has to be eaten.

There are problems with eating while riding, namely, as you are breathing harder than normal, anything with crummy bits carries a danger of choking since loose crumbs can make their way into the airways. After a quest taking years I discovered that the best long-distance food is marzipan. This has the advantage not only in that it doesn't produce crumbs but also it has perfect consistency to be pushed to the outside of the mouth on either side almost like a hamster. This means it can be chewed on while breathing heavily even on high output stretches such as climbs. The other benefit is that energy content is incredibly high. Commercial energy bars also have a high-energy content but these must be tested on a training ride to monitor your personal affinity with them.

There is also the phenomenon of commercially available preparations that are promoted as agents for greater efficiency. A popular one among these is creatine phosphate. The theory behind this relies on a pivotal reaction that drives all energy transfer carried out by an enzyme called adenosine triphosphate, where the phosphate group acts as carrier in a reaction chain. The idea is that the phosphate in the creatine will boost this enzyme and increase power output. There is firstly the problem that the substance is consumed orally, after which it is digested then carried in its constituent parts to organs in the body before being assimilated, and secondly that the enzyme is already in adequate supply. It travels through the bloodstream before arriving at the liver to be dealt with. The blood is actually quite a delicate part of your overall biology and anything that risks causing an imbalance, especially in pH, is best left alone. The pH (acidity) of the blood is 7.4, but if it dropped to 7 or rose to 7.8 you would be dead in minutes. Luckily we have a buffering mechanism to prevent this. Be warned though, the more we stress it the closer it is to breaking down. A family friend died from using bicarbonate of soda to control his ulcer; his blood had become alkaline. No one could save him. Don't take chances on products that are not tested or regulated as drugs. These will normally have a more negative impact than positive and, surprise, surprise, are commercial products sold for profit. Remember: qui bono?

IN BRIEF

We need to be as obsessive with our nutrition planning as we are with our training plan, or bike set-up. Like every other aspect of training, preparation is the key to making our diet work to deliver the best in terms of nutrition. The food we consume is not only to balance our hunger but to provide the best mix of nutrients, proteins and carbohydrates through which a hard-working cyclist can allow their bodies to repair and build from the training and event programmes they follow.

- Food labelling can be complicated but it is well worth taking the time to understand really what is in the pre-prepared and processed foods you consume
- I swear by preparing food for the return from a hard training effort and have always considered this to be a key part of my training cycle
- There can be no disputing that natural foods are best
- The human body is conditioned to a consumption and digestion process which begins with mastication (chewing) before food enters the digestive tract
- Preparing food in advance to an event is important as your body balance can be challenged by consuming a foodstuff which is not part of your regular dietary intake
- Processed foods contain many hidden dangers such as artificial ingredients, inflated salt and sugar contents – remember the lawyers' old adage: *let the buyer beware*

13

Illness and other matters

Illness, injury and other setbacks can and will happen to most riders. This quite often seems to strike at the worst possible times when we are making good progress towards our goals. It often seems that we are powerless over our fate, that there is little we can do apart from stretching and eating well and that what is coming our way is unavoidable fate. To a large extent this is true, but a lot of illness and injury can be traced back to a place and a time that could have been avoided. If you go ice-skating and twist a knee, then clearly a good walk would have been a better choice after the fact. Weighing up risk and choosing alternatives is a good way of avoiding injuries.

When it comes to illness and infections, then, it is not possible to avoid all risks, and sometimes it is inevitable that you will have to spend time with someone who is carrying a cold or flu. We can do what we are able to avoid these people in a social environment though, and it is common practice for me to quietly move carriage on a train if I hear someone coughing and sneezing as an example of avoidance. If I have a serious event coming up, I will be sure to enquire about a possible visitor's health in advance, and if they are down with an infection, I will be kind-hearted enough to forgo their company so they can get a better rest.

Also, when it comes to infections, avoiding airborne viruses in the workplace or public places is impossible, but a large percentage of infections are actually contracted through touch, food or drink. Being careful about washing hands before eating and trying to break away from the habit of rubbing eyes or scratching your nose or any hand-to-face contact at all, especially during virus rich activities like using keyboards, will cut down your chances considerably. Another source of germs is the water bottle. In any slightly damp surface, spray from the road will come up from your front wheel and some of it will be deposited on the spout of your bottle. There is not much we can do about this in an event, but when we are out training on our working bike there will be very little spray coming up and here is another very good plus point for the use of full-length mudguards. If you dropped a sandwich on a grubby country road, you would not dream of picking it up and eating it, yet we will tolerate the equivalent from our water bottles. When riding in a group this misty spray will end up all over the place anyway, but if I see that my water bottle has been contaminated, I will give one bottle a quick squirt with another before using.

I deviate at this point onto another matter, which is the act of riding one-handed while rummaging for food or using a water bottle. I always cringe when I see riders keeping one 'steering hand' on the drops or even the hood of the brake lever. This is a dangerous practice since if you hit a bump or have to brake for whatever reason then the front end of the bike is completely off balance and the force on the handlebar will push the front wheel sideways. I have even seen that one steering hand being freed from the handlebars completely by a bump – not pretty. The correct way is to put your steering hand on top of the bar with your fingers forward and your thumb behind before using your other hand. That way your bike will remain stable over the largest of bumps and because your thumb is behind there is no way your hand can be knocked downward off the bars. Riding one-handed can never be as safe as with both hands, but knowing this means we can be better prepared. Firstly, choose your moment as best as you can on a flat and straight section, and secondly, give yourself room from a rider in front so you can better see what is going on ahead and have more room and time to react. In the case of emergencies (if someone else crashes for this reason in front of you, for example), grip the water bottle or food in your teeth and go to both brake levers.

We tend to use the same hand for drinking and eating on a bike and therefore our bar hand should always start off on the same spot. I highly recommend fitting a secondary lever at that spot on the tops in order that you can slow down safely when riding one-handed. The extra weight is about 50g! It is also very useful when signalling at junctions.

On the subject of contracting infections there is another side to the equation. Our body's own defence mechanism, the immune system, is what will ultimately determine whether an infection becomes a full-blown illness, a few days of feeling a bit under the weather, or it is totally resisted from the start. One thing we can do is not let our immune system be in a position where it is weakened and therefore more likely to be overwhelmed. It is current scientific thinking that getting chilled in itself will not cause an infection, but if a virus is present then being chilled will certainly give it a good chance to gain a foothold. A lot of viruses are embedded within our cells and when an opportunity arises such as a drop in core temperature then the latent virus

SEX IS ONLY A LIGHT
WARM-UP

becomes active. The best thing is to prepare for situations where this might happen and either avoid them or be equipped to deal with the situation. A common place to get chilled is on group rides where you could be waiting for ages before even getting started and then when you are riding there can be a spate of punctures, ruining the rhythm of the ride and the opportunity to build up body temperature.

The first thing is to always carry a skullcap and a good quality cape and as soon as there is a hold-up, put them on. The second thing that I can quite often do is to kindly fix somebody's puncture for them. That way I get to be active rather than sedentary, and I also get to pump up the tyre which helps generate heat, especially with the silly mini-pumps of today. Most of the time in cold weather I also carry a touring cape, which is an old-fashioned poncho type thing. If you have a puncture or mechanical in the countryside in a downpour, then even with a standard cape you are going to get pretty wet and cold. You can buy cheaper and lighter versions that are intended for festivals but are pocket sized and perfect for stops. Make sure you get one with a hood.

There is a place and time where a lot of riders get chilled inadvertently, even in reasonably good conditions, actually, more so in good weather conditions. That time is just after an event where the rider feels warm, hot even. They get chatting to team-mates and friends still in sweaty racing clothes. By the time they realise they are getting cold, they are cold. This is the worst time to have a sudden drop in body temperature just after pushing the body so hard, and the best thing is to get changed right away. Basically, keep walking while you are talking and don't allow yourself to be drawn into conversation.

Places where your chance of becoming ill as a result are pubs and clubs that are really loud. Not because there are necessarily more germs on the go but in order to communicate you more or less have to shout and that in turn gives you a dry and slightly rough throat, the perfect landing place for a germ with aspirations of colonisation. Other than not going out at all or being untalkative, you can take a sip of glycerine now and then, but be sure to have only the tiniest sip and work it back to your throat to keep it moist; don't be fobbed off at the chemist with cough syrup or glycerine with honey or some other mix that doubles its implied value – it has to be pure glycerine. This is a must for your kitbag or beside the turbo if you suffer from dry throat during rides. Gargling with an antiseptic mouthwash at the end of an evening could be the difference between a good and a bad season, especially if you have been in a 'shouty' environment.

Lastly, the difference between feeling a bit lethargic and full-blown infection can be listening to your body and what it is trying to tell you. It ties in with what I wrote about recovery and how it can vary at different

PERSEVERANCE, HOPE & TRUST.

times. If your body is trying to fight off an infection, then it is going to divert resources from recovery to the front line. It would take a day or more of incubation time before you start feeling under the weather. It is at this point that you might be lining up a good session. Your decision whether to batter on regardless or listen to your body and hold back could be the difference between being properly ill or recovering. A lot of times there are no other symptoms other than being 'under the weather' and recovering slowly from the last ride. When proper symptoms do appear, like a runny nose, then the battle has already been lost. Sometimes, of course, we are unaware of it and just think we took a strangely long time to recover from our effort. This is another reason why strict training schedules and full racing diaries are not always good.

> ## the first post-illness ride has to be done and it is unrealistic and unnecessary to ride at exactly the same output that you were doing before illness struck

No matter how careful we are we do get ill sometimes. When we do then all we can do is rest well, keep our stretching programme going and eat well until we get better. The net result is that when we get back to training it seems that we have lost so much fitness. It may seem that way but the very fact of being ill has the effect of slowing down the decline of our aerobic physiology compared to not having exercised for that same period of time. The thinking on this phenomenon, which is purely anecdotal it must be said, is that where exercise is a stress on the body, then illness is also a stress that retards recovery from previous efforts but also retards the process of physiological change that would normally see a sedentary athlete become out of condition.

Nonetheless, when just over an illness, we still feel sluggish and not up to pace. There is no way or point of putting this across gently, you are going to feel seriously sluggish on your first ride back. Get over it, get on with it and get it over with! The bottom line is that the first post-illness ride has to be done and it is unrealistic and unnecessary to ride at exactly the same output that you were doing before illness struck. When you are ill it seems like forever and we are always desperate to get back to riding, but the fact is that we need to wait till our bodies have recovered. The consequence of snatching at it too early is almost always an extension of how long we are ill and an even longer wait to get back to the performance level we had before.

Allowing a similar period of time as the illness in order to return to previous form is a realistic and structured plan, although I stress again that you must not plan set sessions on set days. Recovery can sometimes be a lot quicker than that and anything better is a bonus. Since part of the remit of this book is training and riding within a social environment then may I suggest that the time spent not being debilitatingly ill could be spent doing things and going places with partners or children when you would otherwise be riding. Relationships have to be based to a degree on compromise and although verbalising it would undermine the benefits of doing this, you are effectively storing up credits that will help reduce any resentment that can result in you spending a lot of time away from home on future events.

When it comes to relationships and other matters, there exists in the world of sport the belief that abstinence from sex will improve your sporting performance. This idea is more based on the theory that having sex will somehow take something away from your focus and energy for an event. This became the established norm in the world of boxing and spread to other sports. It is primarily aimed at the male athlete and it is still the case that WAGs (wives and girlfriends) are barred from sleeping with their footballer husbands and partners during major events.

Let us take the view from the perspective of the partner of an amateur cyclist who is dead set on celibacy for a prescribed period of time. I have known riders who abstain for a week or more, not just the night before. From that perspective not only does the cyclist disappear for ages at a time but the partner does not even get any action! Having sex does not even consume that much energy in relation to cycling. A heart-rate monitor will show that it really only equates to a light warm-up. Some time ago I was asked my opinion on this by a French magazine and my answer is the same as it was then: 'It makes no difference – as long as it doesn't make you late for the start.'

In other areas of this manual I have made reference to sports massage. My observation is that massage means different things to different people. A lot of riders say they just feel better for it, others say it relaxes them and still others insist it is essential for their muscles to feel better and hastens recovery. Either way, there is an emotional connection and, hence, benefit for these riders. After all, a perceived benefit is an actual benefit. If you think you feel better, then you do feel better.

There is a cost aspect both in money and more importantly in time. Most riders have to travel to a trusted masseur or masseuse as well, which further adds to the time spent there. That eats into time that could be tight after work or spent on an actual bike ride, or it may result in you getting to bed later than you would normally, with the consequent rest and recovery cost. My opinion is that each rider has to do their own cost-benefit analysis and decide if massage is worth it.

131

There is one factor that you must add into the equation. That is that massage will have almost zero benefit in the quest for suppleness and flexibility. If you undertake massage already, then you will still have to follow the stretching programme I laid out in Chapter 10. You will still have to come back from massage and do stretching. If you do not undertake massage already, then I would say that massage will do no harm and can be nice, and I advise strongly that if you decide to give it a go, it cannot be allowed to impinge in any way on your suppleness programme.

I finish by reminding you that part of our human character is to choose that which is easy over that which is hard, and I do realise that there is a lot of information and new ways of training put forward here to undertake. I too am not immune to procrastination and of slipping back into old and easier ways. Part of the human character is also perseverance, hope and trust. Perseverance will take you to the eventual benefits that you hope to realise.

Your health and welfare is vital. Learn to listen and feel what your body is saying to you. Take the time to get into a zone where you can have the moment to seek out the messages your body is communicating.

IN BRIEF

Your health and physical welfare is vital. Learn to listen, feel and respect what your body is telling you. Personal hygiene can be the key to avoiding illnesses like the common cold. Take the necessary precautions to minimise contact and exposure to colds and other viruses. If you do succumb to illness, let it run its natural course and do not rush back to full training to soon.

14

Selection

Being selected to represent your country may be the furthest thing from your mind. You may be middle-aged and in full-time employment but the world of sport has changed so much in recent times that there are world championships for masters of all ages where riders represent their countries. World masters championships are organised into five-year age categories with world champion status being awarded to each winner in the different age groups. On the other hand you may be a hardcore young rider with ambitions of great victories. Either way you will not achieve your dream of riding for your country or winning at the international level unless you get 'selected'.

What you have to consider is that your competitors for selection are fundamentally no different from you. Are you not just as qualified as they are on that basis? That was my rationale when deciding to attack the all-time one hour record in 1993. Assuming you train the best that you can and are improving your performance through other measures I have discussed then being selected to ride at regional level is an absolute necessity in the process of becoming a top-level cyclist. Rarely has an athlete been chosen at national level that has not previously proved themselves to be selectable material at a regional level. Riding at regional level in races improved me because I was thrown into a situation where I was struggling just to get by.

If you want to race at any level, you have to be noticed by the selectors. There may be other riders with similar results to you, but standing out is not simply a matter of good results and consistent performance. It is a complex mix of potential end ability, team suitability and politics. This is a world apart from the purity of sporting ability alone. It is best to think of selection as a distinct but necessary pursuit detached from your sporting endeavors.

The problem most athletes have is that they assume that, firstly, the selector sees their results and, secondly, that results alone decide who will be selected. The most important thing to realise is that there is not a computer program for selection – this is a decision made by a human being and is often not completely objective. The advent of sports institutes and set guidelines means that certain criteria need to be met before an athlete can even be considered for selection, and in the case of timed events like individual pursuit an actual time cut based on temperature and air pressure is set. Despite this, with several athletes to choose from, more subjective decisions need to be made by key individuals in the selection process.

Being selected to ride at regional level is vitally important because this is the stepping stone to self improvement not only because of better and tougher competition, but also because national selection will rarely happen as a single leap. The thing to remember about being selected at a regional or even local level is that the subjective decision will have less of an influence on direct results and more a bearing on what an individual thinks you are capable of in the future. They may assess you as a person as much as your performance, in terms of whether you will fit into a team set-up or get along with other team members.

It is clear that getting selected is a direct result of your performances, and being the best athlete you can be is the absolute most important thing. That said, being chosen is a huge part of that long-term improvement, so any event you take part in has to be looked at as a gateway to getting picked. It seems like the wrong ambition in itself above the goal of winning events, but this has to be your attitude since not being selected leaves participation in domestic racing at whatever level you can enter as an individual or club team as your only option.

Competing at the highest level that you can allows you access to a lot of advantages. Being selected on a frequent basis means that you will end up receiving equipment and financial support that you would not otherwise get. Some employers will look upon selection as being a good reason to allow time off that would not be granted simply if you had entered an event. The biggest advantage of all is experience. No amount of coaching or reading is going to make up for actually being in the thick of the action. A good example of this is the echelon (a diagonal line out in road events to deal with crosswinds) – most club riders will never have been involved in one of these since they only tend to be implemented in higher level events.

If you are thinking that selection is going to be a target of yours, then you need to have a game plan. It is important to point out that seeking selection is a competitive event in itself. You are competing against your fellow riders for the few places that are available so it is morally acceptable to maximise your chances against those other riders within the bounds of fair play. You

TIP THE
BALANCE
SLIGHTY IN
YOUR FAVOUR

have to be focused on endearing yourself and selling yourself to those who have the power of selection.

The first thing you have to consider is acquiring the right platform to set about getting your best results and having these results noticed by the people that matter. That means you have to analyse what any club can offer in terms of sponsorship, training rides, other team members and what contacts they have with governing bodies. Chances are you are involved in a club already, but if so, you have to question the cost of loyalty if you discover there is a much better club you can be involved with. The other aspect of club membership that a lot of cyclists do not appreciate is that you can compete for one club and be a 'secondary' member of another. I was in this position for several years and most reasonable people will see that it is possible to display loyalty to the club by continuing as a secondary member.

A factor in choosing your competitive club is how strong its media and internet presence is. It is an oft-spoken phrase 'the results will speak for themselves'. Well, actually the reporting of the results will speak for themselves. If you join a club with a large pool of riders, then there will, most likely, be a series of closed events – events just for club members. A club with a strong media presence can get those results into the mainstream press, on its own website and social networks such as Facebook and Twitter. This can matter when it comes to being talked about as a strong rider and selling yourself to the selectors. Club events would rarely be considered in a selection process but the connection of one person to any other in sport is much closer than you may think. Gossip about who has good form never does any harm.

As far as performance goes it is not just the final placings that matter. Sitting in the slipstream all day and lunging to a good result in the finishing straight might not be as impressive to the selector as a solo attack. What does get noticed is if the race is not going right for you or you are having a bad day, and whether you make a decision to abandon or continue racing. Throwing races gets easier the more you practise it, but is a bad idea unless a particular situation is completely hopeless. In a selection event it doesn't send a good message. Don't forget that the selector is not just looking at how good you are today but how good you can be. Champions are etched from tenacity and a determination not to give up. Display those traits and you help your cause. Let's face it, if I was the selector and I saw you climb off, I would be thinking to myself: 'What would that rider do on a cold, wet and windy Tuesday afternoon – train, or leave it until tomorrow?'

As far as dealing with the selectors is concerned it is a great move to contact them directly. If you have a few good results under your belt either this season or last, then do not hesitate. You have to ask for the information that you need, namely, the events that will be looked at for selection purposes. The ideal thing is to write or email initially with your ambitions and best

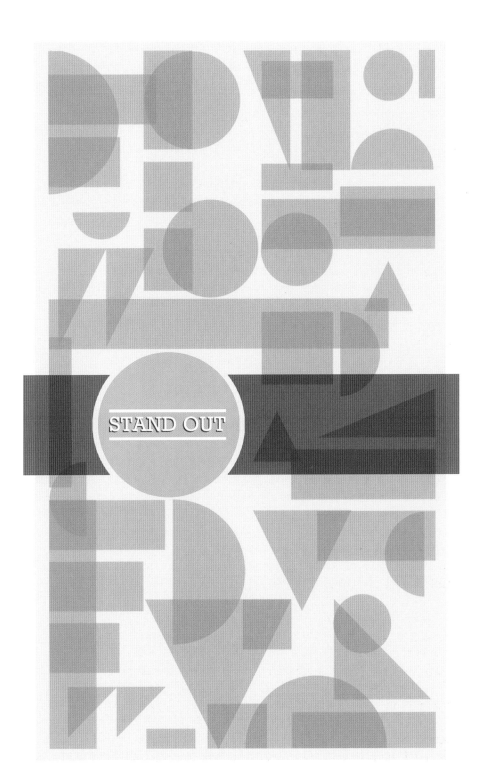
STAND OUT

results to date. You do not want to be too in depth at this stage since what you really want is a person-to-person conversation. You have to tread a line between being humble and confident, but the most important thing is to be honest from the start about your form, your strengths, your weaknesses and your ambitions. Depending on what your event is you may have to ride other events that are not your strong point, so it is important to make it clear that you are up for doing your best at all of them, but that your ultimate goal is being the best that you can in one specific discipline. You must be prepared to listen to what the selector needs from their riders.

This done, you need to plan your season around those events with the club you choose to ride for. I remind you at this point that although selection is the overriding goal it is not the end goal. The end goal is being the best you can possibly be in your sport. It is important to never state that your goal is selection since it sounds like you think that is more important than the competition itself. You have to be on your guard against this from your own performance perspective. It is better to state an aim that obviously requires selection anyhow.

the bar will play a huge roll in your future opportunities

It is possible to increase your chances by being sensible and focused on social factors. It is extremely difficult for some people to be completely impartial with others they know on a personal basis, no matter how hard they try. That is why jurors cannot judge someone they have previously met. Sport is one of those activities where your opportunities and your future are decided by people that you can interact and socialise with – buy drinks for – at events and off-season dinners. Use these opportunities to your advantage!

This may seem like cheating on your rivals, but do you not think some of them are in the same game? The fact is that if you can seek out the selectors and get them interested in following your results then this has to be better than not making any contact at all. It is a fact that who knows whom and who likes or dislikes whom has an influence on decision making no matter how small. When you are selected to take part in an event this involves a lot of hanging around together and it is only human to want to hang out with people that you like. The name of the game is to try and be one of those people. Remembering that results come first, there is an opportunity to tip the balance slightly in your favour.

The easiest way to get that advantage is to join the right club with connections and to go to as many out-of-season dinners and gatherings as possible. Do research on those you are targeting and be interested in them as people. These events may be your first chance to speak to the selectors and make a good impression, so rule number one is not to drink too much. The question of what the selection races are is a good opener to a conversation. Be generous when it comes to buying drinks and talk about things not related to cycling – family, hobbies, pets, etc. Don't forget that this is a dress rehearsal for the days spent together at the selection events themselves. It is a good idea to Google the selectors before engaging in conversation but, of course, you should never divulge this fact to them. It is best to follow rule number one of the 'gold-digger' – never tell anyone you are a gold-digger! In other words don't let them know you are at that event and chatting away to them primarily as part of your selection campaign.

> ### if a rider is mouthy and out of line, then it doesn't take long for a reputation to suffer in a sport that is as close-knit as road or track cycling

Should you be lucky enough, or rather, dedicated enough to be selected then the next thing you have to keep in mind from minute one of being in the selection event is getting reselected. You have to be honest at this point about your true form and experience. As long as the selectors know that you have long-term ambitions and are willing to struggle through to be that good, no matter the result this time, then you are in with a good shout. Nonetheless, the bar will play a huge role in your future opportunities. Usually after an event you stay over and travel the next day. That evening involves a meal and the bar. No matter how exhausted you are you must be at that bar until the end. In the immediate aftermath of the results, opinions will be formed on who has winner potential and who doesn't. If you are there until the close, then the benefit is that you get to know these people better and you show that you are up for a social at other events.

Another important thing you have to do is learn as much about your sport and the rules of your sport as you can. This is something you would do if you were in business. Get a hold of the constitution of your governing body and read it – all of it. Get a hold of a paper or internet copy of the rules of racing, both nationally and internationally. This is a lot of work but it is a side of your sport that most riders remain ignorant of. When you grasp this knowledge you will be able to converse with those who run our sport much better. This not only gives you the ability to have that bar conversation at a deeper level but it will also arm you to make the most of the rules in situations that would normally leave you baffled as to what to do.

Ignorance of the rules has often let me down in my career, and it happens at the point of feeling you have been wronged yet don't know the procedure to deal with it. Although not related directly to the selection process, knowing how to appeal – and just as importantly – how to counter-appeal is very important as it can change the final result and aid your campaign for selection. It is worth saying that in all of these interactions that usually take place in domestic racing, that is, races you can enter, you deal with officials who are unpaid and give up their time for the love of the sport. It is important to respect this, and it is worth saying that if a rider is mouthy and out of line, then it doesn't take long for a reputation to suffer in a sport that is as close-knit as road or track cycling. Politeness and respect pay dividends for you both in terms of reputation and in terms of how you feel about yourself. It is good discipline. Behaviour that makes you feel better as a person also makes you train better and sleep better. Always try to conduct yourself in a gentle manner when you are not actually competing.

IN BRIEF

To sum it up, you have to train to be the best athlete you possibly can be. You have to engage with selectors and be both pleasant and honest. You have to almost stalk them without them knowing they have been Googled and targeted at social events. Above all you have to remember that form comes before flattery, but playing the selection game really can tilt the balance in your favour.

15

The dichotomy of sport

From a young age most of us are brought up to be civil in a civilised, ordered society. That means waiting your turn, thinking of others and considering how our actions affect others without being brutish and self-centered. Competitive sport, by its very nature, where to win is the ultimate goal, necessitates behaviour that is the absolute opposite to this.

In normal life we let people go ahead of us in doorways and queue politely. This is taught to us from a young age to the point that we don't think openly about our actions. It becomes our very nature to not barge and snatch. Our conditioning prevents us from rugby tackling our way to grab the last cake on a supermarket shelf even though we really want it for ourselves.

Competitive sport is one of the few activities where it is not only acceptable to behave this way, but it is at the very heart of the activity itself. A lot of sportspeople know they love competing but cannot quite get a total handle on why that is. The truth is that the momentary freedom from this social conditioning is central to the exhilaration that sport can deliver. When you realise this then working on doing more of it can only bring improved results and more enjoyment of the socially unacceptable lunge to grab what you want – victory – or as close to it as possible. This is not being a bad citizen – this is being a good competitor.

The word 'sport' has many connotations and varied interpretations, some of which imply being a 'good sport' – in other words, acting in a gentlemanly fashion – are part of being a sportsperson. These values are important and worthwhile but the action end of sport is a different matter altogether. Here, you are at the polar opposite of 'good sport'. This is more akin to 'total sport', which I would liken very much to the phrase 'total war'.

This is the dichotomy (that is, it involves sharply distinguished opposites). Until the countdown to an event we are obliged to adhere to social conditioning even to the extent of chatting to the timekeeper, officials or other riders. Then you must eschew all of that and quickly become what is known in normal society as a sociopath – a person who follows their own ambition at whatever cost to others. There is a test that has been used to test narcissism by psychologists for some time now. The question is as follows. You are a guy at a funeral of a family member and meet a woman you become infatuated with. She leaves, and you can't find out who she is. Two weeks later you kill your brother. Why?

I have asked this to many true winners and to those whom until now have been rather ordinary. When I appeal to the mindset of what the goal is (meeting this woman again) then real 'getters' get the answer pretty quickly – that there will be another funeral and perhaps another chance. That is not acceptable in society, but if you look at Sir Chris Hoy winning the 2012 World Keirin Championship he dived through a tiny space and went under the other riders in a move that no coach would ever countenance. He won, because he was focused totally on the goal at all cost. Sir Chris is not a sociopath and is a genuine 'good sport' in real life and one of the politest, nicest people you could ever meet, as is the case with many 'winners'.

I hope it makes you think about what is it that changes in them when it comes to the action end of competition. What is it that I have not been able to access to its full potential? The answer is not what you can't do but what we will naturally do had we not been socially conditioned not to. Take the example of a toddler who has not yet been conditioned. We have all seen a young child on his/her back having a tantrum. What that says is 'I will keep kicking and screaming until I get what I want – my goal'. This is conditioned out of us pretty quickly.

In a sporting sense, this is equivalent to thinking I will pedal as hard as I like and manoeuvre as I like till I get what I want. That is what society rejects as a behaviour pattern and yet what victory in cycling demands. The problem is that one mindset is in mainstream society yet the opposite is a necessity for sporting winners.

I speak in other chapters about our goal not being to beat others but for our goal to be the best that we can be for ourselves. This is true, but in sport to be the best we can be we *must* beat others. There is a dichotomy within a dichotomy. Are we about beating others or being the best we can for ourselves, and must we be sociopaths in competition against the conditioning of society to be polite and restrained? The answer is to be the best we can be for ourselves by beating others and by being able to ignore our social conditioning during the competitive event.

The first step in achieving a different mindset is accepting that an alternative is necessary. After that, though, just deciding that you will be ruthless won't go very far in undoing a lifetime of civil behaviour. It helps to understand that this is not being nasty to your competitors and possibly your friends – this is behaving in a way that they actually want and appreciate. Let's face it, if you are involved in a sprint for a town sign and the others half-heartedly kind of went for it you would be a bit disappointed. On the other hand if it was full-on and you got boxed into the gutter (but not decked) and you had to come the long way round in an elbow-to-elbow confrontation you would prefer that, even if you get beaten. If you understand at a deep level that ruthlessness is actually the opposite of nasty, that it is actually kind and generous, then you can go a long way to offsetting civil conditioning. After all, not being nasty is a real-time inhibitor, so only think of sporting ruthlessness as kind, generous, selfless and good from now on.

So if this ruthlessness is not nasty, then exactly how can it be useful and how do I get to it? You need to grasp the idea that this is not a change of behaviour pattern – it is the adoption of an entirely new psyche. If you try to subjugate your conditioning to not barge, to think of others, etc., then you are just subjugating an existing subjugation. You have to move to a new mindset, a wild untamed mindset where the only restriction is not causing excessive danger to others.

Actually, it's mainly not even about others and more about reaching an ultimate level of what you are capable of. Although group racing is a good example of where narcissism and ruthlessness will help, this new mindset is also needed for time trials and training. We need to overturn generations of civilising and years of personal conditioning to reach back to a mindset that can best be described as primal. Become, literally, a controlled maniac. This is a Dr Jekyll and Mr Hyde of difference. If both of these characters had a fight, I know which one I would back, even as physical equals. Put another way, which one would be quicker in a time trial or win a match sprint or any 'sporting' contest? Learn to become that person.

You don't just unleash a ruthlessness that you are kind enough to share with riders round about you or to grab that turbo target you want to make you feel good. You unlock the desperation and tenacity of a hungry hunter. Think: 'I will clamber over any obstacle with my last gasp to get what I want'. Think: *'mine – it's mine'*.

That is all very good, but there is just one slight problem: we have to go from civil to primal pretty quickly and then back again. Of course, there is the challenge of reaching back to a primal mindset in the first instance. It has to be said that being in a primal mindset from the very outset is not necessary. In fact it is better in most competitive and training situations to ride on good focus, effort and control until the point at which mental fortitude is needed.

Take for example a turbo-trainer effort of say 20 minutes. The first ten minutes are not easy but it is not necessary to drain your psychological secret weapon. It is best kept till the moment you must not be defeated or worse still, give up, because the civil mind tells you that you cannot do any more. That is the point when you need to be ready to be 'hunter', because nothing is more important than nailing success at your goal. More specifically, because nothing is more important than your self-gratification and *your* feeling of satisfaction and respect. Hunt it down minute by minute and take it – because it's *yours*. The same goes for a time trial or when you are halfway up a hill climb.

All of this may sound a bit extreme but it only works because there is always more within us than we think there is. Take the case of a maniac who resists restraint by four other men, yet in a state of sanity and with martial arts training could not put up such resistance. Even in the playground fight or pub brawl we have been conditioned to be civil. Primal man would rarely punch – he would mostly gouge, bite and strangle.

OK, assuming you buy into it, how about training to tackle the dilemma of fighting and sport – civil and primal in one brain. Here is a great start, and yes, I have done this. Have an adult tantrum. I mean full-blown and moving on to fit or seizure level of unconditioned output of thrashing energy and noise. Do it on your back and wear lace-up boots with a good heel that will not kick off. Elbow pads and helmet are good extras as well if you really are going to do this properly. Then again you could just do this in your bed.

You probably won't though, or you will plan to do it another time – because it seems so wrong! That is the point though – it is wrong in an adult civil society. If you really want to challenge your conditioning, then get on down there and even just do a mini-tantrum. You might do this but you probably won't – the fact that it feels so wrong must highlight in your thinking self the reality of your conditioning. Nothing else that I have tried has come anywhere near as close to imitating the energy and attitude of the primal mind. If you are brave enough to overcome the false feelings of fear, anxiety, rejection and social stigma and actually give it a go, then more than likely your first attempt will be inhibited and feeble. Those feelings have no logical justification since nothing bad will happen and you are following the instruction of a book. Nonetheless they exist and have been the founding bedrock of your conditioning before you can even remember. At least acknowledge their existence as part of your journey to overcome them.

Can you imagine being at a wedding reception and walking straight up to the cake and scooping out part of it with your bare hands and stuffing it in your mouth? Of course not! That is, though, what your primal self would want to do. You would be inhibited by fear, anxiety and the thought of social stigma. Isn't that what you are behaving like if you really go for it and switch your team-mates into the gutter (not decking them though) and elbow your way past them using the mindset and energy of the tantrum to outsprint them to the town sign. And of course you would not do that with commitment

WINNING
- IS -
THE ULTIMATE GOAL

since those very deep-rooted feelings will be present to inhibit you. No matter how much your conditioned thinking self tries to be uninhibited, you still are at some level unless you can find some other way to become truly primal.

I talked at the very start about how specific training gets specific results. It is possible to train a primal psyche by practising turning it on when you most need it. There are two main areas where this can be done. One is open racing or climb rides where you must defeat the other riders in order to reach a specific place ahead of them and thus scoop up the taste of success. The other is time-trialling and solo training where you must defeat the thoughts of the civil mind in order to enjoy success.

In the case of the group race all you can do is be as ruthless (for the good of the others) and primal as you can and analyse afterwards how close to being truly ruthless and energised as in a tantrum you have actually been. Similar can be said of the time trial and turbo effort in that, at the point where a civil mind would collapse and give up, you go primal and use tantrum-like energy to hunt down success. In both cases you are training your ability to go from civil to primal and only practice and analysis will improve this.

The biggest and deepest emotion we try to overcome is fear. Fear is the umbrella emotion that many others shelter under. Shyness, for example, is the fear of the consequences of being outgoing. Fear does not exist of itself. It is taught to us as a consequence of actions or events. The fear of dying is one that does not exist in a primal hunter as a consequence of effort. Only in recent society has effort been associated with pain, with physical damage and thus possibility of death. We all know about the guy running the first marathon to deliver a vital message – and dying from his effort! You might not think it's there, but it is in your consequence-driven civil mind. Death is a strong demotivator.

The perception of pain serves the very useful purpose of telling your brain that there is a part of your body in danger. This ranges from discomfort through to extreme agony. The instinctive reaction is to get away from whatever it is that causes that danger. Your thinking self does not compute the logic of pain equalling damage, injury or even death – it is your hard-wired subconscious self that does this. The effect is that as you try to push yourself to the highest level of effort there is a battle between your motivated self striving for your best performance and your protective subconscious trying to limit damage as it recognises the feedback of effort as pain. This is most acute at the later stages of a solo effort like a time trial or individual pursuit on the track.

What we are really dealing with is the conscious and subconscious mind being in disharmony over just how far you should push the limit. I used to imagine the effort I was doing being like a scene from an old silent movie where a steam boiler is expanding as though it is made of rubber and the

- PUSH THE NEEDLE -

needle is actually bending past the danger end of the dial. This is how your subconscious interprets your maximal effort as your heart is pounding and you are gasping for breath. In nature we have evolved in an environment where that level of effort would be outputted only as a result of either 'fight or flight'.

It is one thing being a hunter and driving on to overcome prey in a proactive way, but it is another situation to be reactive and either fight or run away to save your life. Then there is the situation where not only is your life in danger but also that of your child. You can imagine this situation whether you have a child or not. Imagine your child had been abducted in a car and you were chasing that car on your bike. Would that be your best ever performance? Of course it would, you think, but if you are physically capable of it, why do you not do that every time?

The answer is it all comes down to fear. It is either internal fear or the lack of 'perceived' external fear that inhibits your performance. When I broke the world hour record in 1993 the very next day after having failed to break it, with a body that was drained by the effort of yesterday, I was driven on by a change in the way I perceived my fears. The truth is that the consequences of failure seemed so dire to me on a personal level that this felt like a fate worse than death itself. The personal issues that led to this analysis are complicated but not relevant to the point. What does matter is that the brief moment of failure on day one and how emotionally painful it actually was led quickly to the decision to go again and thus postpone the failure until after the next attempt.

There were two extreme and rapid psychological changes to my psyche that made it possible for a more tired body to ride further and faster than before. Fundamentally, the monster I was fleeing from (the pain of failure) was considerably larger than I had previously perceived it to be. No one else could see it but I was riding *from* a fate worse than death. There was, along with this, a massive change in my internal fear syndrome, but I will explain more after asking you to consider this question.

I ask you to imagine that from as young as you can remember you were fascinated by space and had a driving ambition to be an astronaut. You were fascinated by space travel and the thought of reaching alien worlds. Imagine you worked hard at school and university driven by this passion. Imagine you became an astronaut – and a good one. Imagine you were one of the most accomplished working for NASA. One day you get a call from the head of space exploration and are asked this question – my question. 'We have developed a space vehicle that will take you guaranteed to Mars, but there is only about a 25 per cent chance you will get back alive – are you up for it?' You will be the first human to walk on a foreign planet. Do you agree to the mission or not. Yes or no?

Most people who can truly empathise with that passion will say yes. The question I really need to ask is why should a passion for a sporting goal be any different in terms of acceptance of the risk of death itself? The answer is that we accept someone taking that risk for space exploration but we see a sporting endeavour as something that is not worth dying for.

That was the other change in my psyche before the second hour-record ride. I was truly willing to accept that I will push the needle on that expanding boiler as far as it will possibly go and accept the consequences – even actual death. I accepted this at the deepest level such that my conscious and subconscious selves were acting as one to rev the engine, the human engine, to the point of explosion. The fear remained, of course, but the consequence of non-restraint became acceptable at a subconscious level. This change led me to change my psyche to a completely new one. One where proactive effort to my true maximum would be employed. I was that hunter. I was a cat cornered by a pack of wolves or a soldier with one grenade attacking a pillbox that was killing my comrades.

In reality my thinking logical self knew that I must truly be willing to die in the quest of my goal in order that my inner self would allow me to get close enough to death to succeed. My thinking self knew that few athletes actually die of effort – and few do. I knew that the only difference this time is attitude. Yes it is a mind game, but it is a mind game that works. It works as a psychological trick to release that fight or flight energy, but there is one catch: you have to do the soul searching to see that you are actually willing to risk dying in the quest to fulfil your passion, your dream. Remember that although you almost certainly will not die, you must truly be willing. Pretending just won't do. If you just cannot accept this, then here is a good moment to decide whether you can continue with the dedication and sacrifices that you and, more importantly, those closest to you must make for you to be the best prepared that you can be. It is also a good moment to mention that if you are willing to risk death for a passion that with the same dedication would earn you millions in business, then it's not about the money. In other words don't take drugs and cheat! This would undermine your passion and therefore your ability to reach to primal energy. That would be like being a soldier in a morally wrong war. Think of the decades to follow of satisfaction or regret!

It is important to know that most sudden athletic deaths are caused by a pre-existing heart defect. I say this because my advice is to have your doctor check out your heart in order to reassure your thinking self that you can play this game with a degree of security of mind. This allows you to adopt this attitude at the deepest level, which then in the course of time becomes ingrained into your subconscious that this is an effort to the point of possible death – but we don't care!

In the course of revealing the fact of two mindsets within all of us acting in different directions, I have written about quite dramatic actions and dramatic changes to the psychological approach to being all that you truly can be. My last question is this: If you are willing to risk death for the pursuit of your dream, then why have you not had a tantrum yet? Think about it, you are willing to risk death and, let's face it, cycling can be quite a dangerous sport anyhow – so what is being out of your comfort zone to start all of this process off in comparison to that?

Get on that mattress and start the process of turning your subconscious into an ally that will help you get access to that primal 'fight or flight' energy that has been denied to you until now. Or, maybe, just cycle for pleasure.

IN BRIEF

Until the countdown to an event you are obliged to adhere to social niceties. Once the race starts you must eschew all of that and become a narcissistic sociopath, following your own ambition at whatever cost to others. 'Going primal' will help you push yourself further than your nice self will allow. Think: 'I will clamber over any obstacle with my last gasp to get what I want'. Think: *'mine – it's mine'*. Undoing a lifetime of civil behaviour is not easy. But this too we can train.

- To offset your civil conditioning, understand at a deep level that ruthlessness is actually the opposite of nasty, that it is generous, encouraging the competitiveness of sport that all participants enjoy
- Your subconscious fears pain and believes that pain will lead to death, but if you embrace death, truly being ready to die racing (although you are very unlikely to die), you will dampen those subconscious brakes
- Fear failure more than death, let fear drive you on as opposed to holding you back
- Try having a full-blown, full-volume toddler tantrum to find your inner narcissist
- Keep that tantrum feeling and teach yourself to turn it on mid-race

Conclusion

Please trust me that this body of honest work is given in the best of spirit. I have been the guinea pig in the quest to refine my training on every level, and I can commend it really does work. Knowledge and understanding is a constant quest. This book is not definitive, and keeping an open mind on new findings and developments is not only a good thing but essential if you are serious in your search for new and better ways to improve your cycling and athletic performance.

Information is the golden thread throughout this book. The more information you compile in relation to your preparation for any chosen event, the better prepared for your task you can become, and this can make the difference between being a club rider and a world champion. My quest as an athlete was always to go into the minute detail in the areas I could influence to affect the outcome to my advantage in terms of my performance. Trust me, if you take care in all aspects of your preparation and performance, you will become an improved cyclist and perform better in your chosen discipline, if that is your goal.

Acknowledgements

Writing this training manual has been something of an epiphany. Having to delve so deeply into my own mind and experiences has been sometimes a profound journey, like travelling through time, to get to the route of my understanding. The objective in writing this manual has always been to take my experiences and present them in a sense that is understandable and relevant to cyclists, all cyclists, in particular those new to the sport or those with a thirst to look for new information. Given I have been cycling for most of my life and that cycling has been central to so much of my life, there was much to trawl over. The times I spent in my relative youth running a cycling shop allowed me to hone skills that became invaluable as I moved from a club cyclist to capturing one of cycling's greatest challenges, the world hour record. Indeed if my cycling education had not included my time involved in running bike shops, I may not have been equipped to build my own bikes. Ditto my fascination with improving performance as an athlete; how to capture the energy your body can output has been a journey that still fascinates, and I hope that some of this translates to the reader.

Now no book is completed in isolation. Thanks are due to many individuals who have been directly and indirectly involved in helping produce *The Obree Way*. My cycling and training education began as a teenager when I begged and borrowed from cycling club colleagues. This was invaluable as it gave me the platform to develop my interest into an all-consuming passion. My eternal gratitude to all the clubs and all the riders who have taken the time and effort to chat to me through the years, discussing technical and athletic issues that have been of great benefit to me. Those early days at the local time trial over cups of tea after the event was time incredibly well spent as I was able to pick the brains of more experienced riders and officials. This sometimes fast-tracked my build of information, allowing me to assess what was best for me. Lots of friends and colleagues have been of great help in the project to bring this publication to life. It is said that writing can be a lonely art – well in this case the help I was afforded really challenges that description.

In no distinct order my personal thanks to: John Beattie (www.bbc.co.uk/blogs/johnbeattie), Brian Palmer of the Washing Machine Post (www.thewashingmachinepost.net), Phil Jones (www.race-pace.net), Richard Moore (www.skysports.com/opinion/0,25219,16299,00.html), Rick Robson (www.cyclesportphotos.com), SNS (www.snspix.com), Neil Scholes, Stephen Weideger; Anne, Euan and Jamie, and to the selfless volunteers who make sport happen.

Photos

Index

Index